What People A~

100+ Native American Women Who Changed the World is a wonderful exploration of female Native American leaders. Through her words, it is clear that Ms. Schaller is dedicated to producing a well-researched and comprehensive representation of our Indigenous mothers, sisters, daughters and friends. Uda, Ms. Schaller, for gifting us with this beautiful collection of stories.

—LaDonna Harris (Comanche)
President and Founder of Americans for Indian Opportunity
(www.aio.org)

This collection of 100+ Native American women movers and shakers has been long overdue. Native American women's stories are a vital part of American history and women's history.

The stories of how these women propelled the culture despite the hurdles they faced is a testament to the spirit within all of us that cries out against injustice, that seeks freedom, that yearns for the betterment of all. Ultimately, these stories do not just encourage Native American women, but they are stories which have the power to resonate within men and women globally for their humanity, their courage, their hope.

—Carole Di Tosti, PhD
http://caroleditosti.brandyourself.com/
http://technorati.com/people/goldensylph/

100+ Native American Women Who Changed the World gives a fascinating glimpse at this continent's women of aboriginal heritage and their largely unheralded contributions. Although virtually unknown to the mainstream societies in which they live, they are no less worthy of recognition.

Historical and contemporary, in fields of enterprise or in voicing appeals to our collective conscience, they have served their tribal communities as well as the larger nations in which they live. This is an eye-opening must-read for all who appreciate diversity and revere justice and equality for all.

—Gini Graham Scott, PhD
changemakers@pacbell.net

"I am so grateful to K.B. Schaller, for drawing our attention to these important Native American heroines who have, in many cases, made the ultimate sacrifice. They have shown us through their contributions that their place in history is well deserved. And they are an example for us to know who we are, and can be, as earth people walking it out in the world."

---**Jane L. Fitzpatrick,**
Author of *Windcatcher: The Story of Sacajawea*

KB Schaller has done a magnificent job of honoring these 100+ fascinating Native American women in this collection, *100+ Native American Women Who Changed the World*. Even from a male viewpoint, I appreciate Ms. Schaller's placing them in posterity where they, indeed, should be. All Native Americans deserve to be regarded with honor and respect. These 100+ Native American women very well represent a proud and powerful nation.

—**Tom Blubaugh**
Author of *Night of the Cossack*

100+ Native American Women Who Changed the World is a great collection of well over a hundred outstanding and accomplished Native Indian women. To see what they accomplished in spite of sometimes having to overcome the obstacles of racism and sexism is an accomplishment in itself.

This book gives credit where it is due to a group long overlooked. Every young Native American Indian woman should have a copy of this book, and every library several copies on its shelf.

—**William "Rattlesnake" Jackson**
Principal Chief, American Cherokee Confederacy

Women generally walk two trails—one is the nurturer of families and the carrier of their stories; the other is a growing recognition of the self, or the desire of one's inner self to achieve a sense of belonging to herself. A longing to develop one's creative energies apart from one's given duties.

I think there also is another aspect of the "divided trail." I am mixed-blood. I was born between two worlds—the Cherokee and European. I was not one or the other. Finding one's invisible self—naming it and giving it identity—has been part of my work.

I had a sense of being under a tarp. Not in the purdah sense, but an inner covering that had to be thrown off to face the nakedness of the inner life questioning who I was and what I was about. I think native women and women in general have to work toward the establishment of self.

100+ Native American Women Who Changed the World helps women to realize and celebrate their own strengths, identities and diversities.

—Diane Glancy (Cherokee)
Playwright, poet, movie director

These excellent stories about Native American women and their contributions not only to Native Americans, but to the whole of American society, are both timely and fascinating. I do hope Ms. Schaller publishes more of them.

—John M. "Doc" Briley, Jr., MD,
Children's author and avid student of American history

Historically, Native American women played a central role in tribal decisions and were highly regarded as the "mothers of nations," because their role was deemed so essential to the perpetuation of culture. Unlike their European counterparts, these women were influential in tribal politics and decision-making, but little was recorded about them and colonization eventually subjugated their authoritative roles. I can't help thinking how much I would've loved to have had books like Schaller's *100+ Native American Women Who Changed the World* when I was young and learning about my Native heritage.

—Sharon Irla (Cherokee),
Painter

Because their accomplishments and contributions are not frequently portrayed by the media, *100+ Native American Women Who Changed the World* serves as an inspiration not only to Native Americans, but to all who value freedom, justice and equality, regardless of ethnicity, race, or gender.

—Alejandro De La Garza
http://chiefwritingwolf.com/

100+ NATIVE AMERICAN WOMEN WHO CHANGED THE WORLD

BY

KB SCHALLER

the Peppertree Press
Sarasota, Florida

Compiled and Adapted by USA Book News
National Best Books Award Winning Author, KB Schaller

All Scripture quotations unless otherwise noted are taken from The Holy Bible (London: Eyre and Spottiswoode Limited), with grateful thanks.

While the author has made every effort to provide accurate internet addresses and other contact data where applicable at the time of publication, neither the publisher nor the author assumes any responsibility for errors or changes that occur after publication.

For information regarding permission,
call 941-922-2662 or contact us at our website:
www.peppertreepublishing.com or write to:
the Peppertree Press, LLC.
Attention: Publisher
1269 First Street, Suite 7
Sarasota, Florida 34236

ISBN: 978-1-61493-216-1

Library of Congress Number: 2013919667

Printed in the U.S.A.

Printed February 2014

"Be ashamed to die before you have won some battle for humanity."

—Horace Mann (1796-1859),
spoken to a college graduation class
a few weeks before his death.

CONTENTS

SINGERS, MUSICIANS AND DANCERS

STORYTELLERS, AUTHORS AND POETS

ATTORNEYS, LEADERS AND POLITICIANS

Artists, Craftspersons, and Designers

PHYSICIANS, NURSES, EDUCATORS AND PUBLIC SERVANTS

SCIENTISTS, ENGINEERS, MATHEMATICIANS

ACTRESSES, DIRECTORS, AND PRODUCERS

MILITARY AND OTHER HEROINES

Athletes and Olympians

AND THOSE WITH WINGS

A SAINT, MINISTERS, AND GOSPEL SINGERS

PREFACE

"MOVERS AND SHAKERS" IS A TERM MERRIAM-Webster defines as people who are active or influential in a field of endeavor. They wield power. They organize. Manage. They challenge and change the order of things, many times, even constructs and beliefs that have been accepted and practiced for generations. More importantly, they are catalysts who awaken zeal and courage within others as when stones are cast upon waters and create ripples that travel far and wide.

There are the Apache 8 women firefighters who proved that they could serve with the best of them.

Grammy Awards winner, Mary Youngblood, defied traditional gender restrictions to master the reed flute.

Eskimo teenager, Alberta Schenck, challenged unfair social dictates and enabled her people to walk in greater freedom and dignity.

The women of WARN confronted giants as they thrust themselves into the fray to remedy a need that only they could at a flashpoint in time.

Not only did spirited pathfinder and trailblazer, Elouise Cobell, establish the first reservation-based, Native-owned national bank, she challenged the United States' mismanagement of trust funds belonging to Native Americans. And won.

Along with other warrior women, Dahteste fought with Geronimo's resistance band. WWII Eskimo Scout, Laura Beltz Wright, was the best sharpshooter in her company, gender notwithstanding.

More recently, Lori Ann Piestewa, in Iraq, paid the ultimate price in service to the United States and was awarded, posthumously, the Purple Heart.

And there are other military heroines. To list them all would be a work unto itself. Therefore, although others are included, even as we honor each of them, this work focuses on the ones who served in eras up to and including World War II, whom history has largely forgotten.

LaDonna Harris founded Americans for Indian Opportunity, a global organization for the economic, political and cultural rights of Indigenous peoples.

Other Native women have captivated our senses through the beauty of music and song. Through clay and beads, grass and fabric. Through drama, poetic voice, and the fluid grace of dance. Athletes have left us breathless as they tested the boundaries of physical endurance and skill.

Not the least in importance are those who sow and till and tend, who water and watch as sprouts grow and yield fruit in due season: "Rez grandmas." Mothers, sisters and aunts, teachers and mentors on whom the world's spotlight has shown less brightly. They are frequently life's unsung heroines who "move" more quietly and "shake" more gently.

But all, through courage, strength, creativity and beauty, effect positive changes in the hearts, attitudes and lives of others.

It is not this author's intent to merely present a catalogue of Native American women, historical and contemporary, but with the help of those who responded to the call for nominees, offer a cross-section of women whose lives, sometimes even with glaring imperfections, created a disrupt in the usual flow of things; who caused society to view its own reflection in a different light. Some, if not most, fit into several categories, which further presents them as multi-faceted human beings with a variety of interests, abilities and accomplishments.

Although this work by no means contains all who deserve to be included here, and the eras and circumstances of their lives sometimes differ, the women in this work are united across the generations in a common struggle for positive change.

May their lives inspire all to reach deeply inward to extract that which is highest within themselves. It is also my hope that these lives will rouse more interest—locally, nationally, and even globally—in uncovering many more of the continent's women of Indigenous heritage, whose stories and contributions deserve to be commemorated.

In conducting Native American research, one may find that dates and timelines are sometimes difficult or impossible to locate. Dates of birth are not held to the same importance as they are in the "mainstream."

The reader, then, must reconcile the subject of the research with other contemporaneous persons or incidents to establish an approximate timeline. What is more important, after all, are the people themselves, and what they accomplished within the context of their time.

The following quote from Mother Teresa, whose wisdom, open hands and compassionate heart toward humanity's neediest transcends the boundaries of time, race and ethnicity, best sums the purpose of this book:

"I alone cannot change the world, but I can cast a stone across the waters to create many ripples."

KB Schaller

In Memory

*Rose M. Jeffers (1928-2011) and
William Thomas (W. T.) Jeffers (1926-2012)
Co-founders, World Changers International (1960)
and Discoveryland! USA (1976), non-profit youth
development and educational organizations for dis-
advantaged Native American children. They dedicated their lives to the betterment of Native American
youths regardless of tribal affiliation.*

I.
ACTIVISTS, PROTESTERS AND WARRIOR WOMEN

In literature and lore, the Native American woman is often depicted as the "Indian Princess" and the shy maiden. Seldom do the media spotlight her in the proactive roles of activist, protester, and warrior.

1 COLLEEN SWAN (B. 1959), ENVIRONMENTALIST

- Placed herself on the frontline to save her village
- Focus of documentary movie, *Kivalina v. Exxon*

Colleen Swan was born and reared in Kivalina, Alaska, a largely Inupiat community. She is a Kivalina City Council member, serves on the Northwest Arctic Borough Economic Development Commission, and for 18 years was Tribal administrator.

She is a member of the federally recognized Alaska Native Village of Kivalina, whose population numbered only 374 persons according to the 2010 census, and 96.3 percent of them are Alaska Natives who depend on ocean life for three-quarters of their food supply. Kivalina is also the only community in the Northwest Arctic Region where people hunt the bowhead whale.

Because sea ice forms later and later each year, there is a growing concern that erosion due to seasonal fall storms has increased the risk of flooding and placed Kivalina among the most eroded of Alaska's villages.

Swan and others blame greenhouse gases emitted from oil, power, and coal companies for climate changes that have caused erosion and other issues, forcing the community, since 1992, to plan to relocate to the mainland. Such a move could cost as much as $400 million, which the tiny community cannot afford, and wants the companies to pay.

In a recent interview on Climate Guest, Swan further expressed flooding concerns, and that an oil spill anywhere in the Arctic would disrupt sea mammal migrations and adversely affect the food source of all people who live on ocean wildlife.

Swan, in 2007, as tribal administrator, and Enoch Adams, Jr., vice-mayor and chairman of Kivalina Relocation Planning Committee (KRPC), made a presentation for both the Native Village of Kivalina and the City of Kivalina to the Alaska Climate Impact Assessment Commission.

Among other concerns, the presentation cited that, over the years, erosion activities have caused the shrinking of the village that resulted in overcrowding, water and sewer concerns, and negative impact on economic development opportunities.

In 2008, the residents filed a federal lawsuit, Native Village of Kivalina v. ExxonMobil Corp., et al., in San Francisco against the companies. It was dismissed in October 2010, and appealed to the Ninth US Circuit Court of Appeals.

In 2011, Swan, who placed herself on the frontline to save her village, became the focus of the documentary movie, *Kivalina v Exxon*. In it, Canadian film director, Ben Addelman, captured the tiny village's struggle against giant oil and gas companies. The film premiered at the Whistler Film Festival and won Best Documentary Award.

Colleen Swan's viewpoints on Kivalina's struggles have appeared in the *Center on Race, Poverty and Environment* newsletter, blogs, and other media outlets.

Swan is a member of Kivalina's Epiphany Episcopal Church, Episcopal Church Women, and a volunteer of Kivalina Search and Rescue. She is also a member of Swan Sisters Gospel Singers, whose recordings include *Silver Trumpet, He's Coming Back Again,* and *Send Your Best Angel.*

Extra: Kivalina

Kivalina is located off the coast of the Chukchi Sea on a barrier reef island in the northwest of the state. The winters are long and cold, the summers, cool. There are no hotels, restaurants, movie theaters, or banks.

The community has a City/Tribal Office, United States Post Office, bingo hall, clinic, laundromat, and several other public facilities. Its water supply is stored in two huge holding tanks and there is no water or sewage service in residential houses.

Visitors who remain for more than a day are usually housed at the school where there are flush toilets and showers. The Kivalina Native Store sells snacks, groceries and other supplies.

There are two churches, Epiphany Episcopal and Kivalina Friends. There are about six cars in the entire community. Besides the Swan Sisters, there are several Christian gospel and other singing groups.

Social outlets are few. For adults, there are gym nights for the athletically inclined and bingo. School-aged children also enjoy gym nights and an occasional adult-sponsored movie or dance. Lately, Inupiaq dance practice is held every other night.

For more about Kivalina, visit City of Kivalina website.

---

2 Winona LaDuke (b.1959), Activist, Author, Environmentalist

- Addressed the United Nations on Indian issues at age 18
- Was vice presidential candidate

Enrolled member of the Mississippi Band, Anishinaabeg (Ojibwe), of the White Earth Reservation (northern Minnesota),

Winona LaDuke was born in Los Angeles, California. Her father, Vincent, was a Native American actor who played supporting roles in Western movies and was also a writer and social activist. Her mother was a Jewish art professor at Southern Oregon University, in Ashland, where Winona was reared.

LaDuke became involved in Native American environmental issues while a student at Harvard University where she met activist Jimmy Durham, a Wolf Clan Cherokee and founder of the International Indian Council.

At age 18, LaDuke addressed the United Nations on Indian issues. She graduated from Harvard in 1982 with a bachelor's degree in rural economic development, and moved to White Earth where she became principal of the reservation's high school.

She earned her MA degree in community economic development at Antioch University, and in 1989 founded White Earth Land Recovery Project (WELRP) to reclaim Anishinaabeg lands promised by a federal treaty in 1867.

Through treaty abrogation, dishonest sales, and theft of property during the past two centuries, however, more than 90 percent of White Earth's original 837,000 acres are currently in the possession of non-Indian people.

LaDuke's activism against such practices entangled her in a long legal battle, but through perseverance, securing grants, and winning a Reebok Human Rights Award (1998), she and White Earth bought back one thousand acres. The goal of WELRP is to buy back thirty thousand more, reestablish tribal ownership and stewardship within the reservation, and to reforest reservation lands.

LaDuke has also served on boards including Greenpeace USA; Honor the Earth; National Native American Foundation; and the Indigenous Women's Network.

Recognized as a strong voice for American Indian economic and environmental issues throughout the United States and worldwide, LaDuke, in 1994 was named by *Time* magazine as one of the nation's fifty most promising leaders under the age of forty.

She was a founding member of Women of All Red Nations

(WARN), formed in the mid-1970s to address issues concerning Indian women and their families, and was twice the United States Green Party vice presidential candidate on the ticket headed by Ralph Nader (1996, 2000).

LaDuke is the author of *Last Standing Woman* (fiction); *All Our Relations* (nonfiction), and a children's book, *In the Sugarbush*.

In 1997, *Ms.* magazine named her Woman of the Year. She won the Anne Bancroft Award for Women's Leadership and, in 2007, was inducted into the National Women's Hall of Fame.

Winona LaDuke is currently Executive Director of White Earth Land Recovery Projects and Honor the Earth, which she also founded.

---

3 ANNA MAE PICTOU-AQUASH (1945-1976), ACTIVIST

- Symbol of the era of Native rights activism

Born to Mi'kmaq parents, Mary Ellen Pictou and Francis Thomas Levi, in a small Indian village in Nova Scotia, Canada, Anna Mae Pictou was the third of four children—two older sisters and a younger brother.

Her father left her mother before she was born, and Anna Mae and her siblings attended school on the Mi'kmaq Reserve where she did well in her studies.

Mary Ellen married again in 1949, this time to Noel Sapier, a Mi'kmaq traditionalist. He was a migrant farmer as were many other Mi'kmaq, and also a craftsman. The family lived without heat, water, or electricity and subsisted on what they were able to harvest—largely, wild turnips and potatoes.

Although a hard-working man, Sapier was unable to earn enough to improve the family's financial status, but he taught the children discipline, instructed them in the traditions of their people, and provided stability in the home.

When he died of cancer in 1956, in the same year, without

warning, Mary Ellen left Anna Mae and her siblings and moved to another Reserve to marry again. The children eked out a living at the only job they knew—harvesting potatoes and berries.

Anna Mae attended school off the reserve, and for the first time ever, encountered blatant racism. Her grades fell, and she eventually dropped out. In 1962 at age 17, she and a friend, Jake Maloney, moved together to Boston, Massachusetts, where Anna Mae found factory work and met other First Nations Canadians and American Indians.

In 1964 and 1965, she gave birth to daughters Denise and Deborah. She and Jake married after the birth of Denise, but the marriage failed and Anna Mae moved back to the Mi'kmaq Reserve.

Sometime between 1968 and 1969 when Native peoples were demanding equal rights, treaty fulfillments, and cultural recognition, Pictou moved to Bar Harbor, Maine, with her daughters and volunteered to teach self-esteem and Native history to young urban Indians.

She became involved in the American Indian Movement (AIM). In 1970, she participated in the group's march in Boston on Thanksgiving Day to protest the Mayflower II celebration. The protest involved the seizure and occupation of the ship, and ignited her passion for Native rights.

Sometime within this timeframe, she met Chippewa artist and activist, Nogeeshik Aquash. She was also instrumental in the creation of the Boston Indian Council. Later renamed the North American Indian Center of Boston, its purpose was to improve Indian life within the city.

In November 1972, she participated in the Trail of Broken Treaties caravan/march on Washington, D.C. After a week of occupying the Bureau of Indian Affairs building, the government promised a point-by-point review of their twenty civil rights demands.

In February 1973, Pictou joined a group of some 200 Oglala Lakota, AIM followers, and other sympathizers who gathered at Wounded Knee near the Pine Ridge Indian Reservation (where on December 29, 1890, 500 United States soldiers killed 300 Minneconjou Ghost Dancers).

The 71-day siege followed a failed attempt to impeach Richard "Dick" Wilson, Tribal president, on charges of corruption and ruling the reservation through intimidation and violence. They further protested broken treaties by the United States Government and demanded a reopening of negotiations.

Anna and Nogeeshik smuggled in food and medical supplies, and also during the siege, were married in a traditional ceremony by a Lakota elder.

When the standoff ended, AIM leaders Russell Means and Dennis Banks were arrested and indicted, while Anna Mae was on her way to leadership within the movement. But events would soon turn tragic for Pictou-Aquash.

On February 24, 1976, her frozen body was discovered by a rancher on the Pine Ridge Reservation. Believed initially to have died from exposure, a second autopsy revealed she had been shot at the base of her skull. It was not until 2003 that arrests were made of those who believed her to be a government informant.

Anna Mae Pictou-Aquash remains a powerful symbol of the era of Native rights activism.

4 Amelia "Amy" Cutsack Trice (1936-2011), Tribal Leader

- Declared "The Last Indian War Against the United States"

Born in Bonners Ferry, Idaho, April 26, 1936, Amelia "Amy" Trice was the daughter of Helen and Baptiste Cutsack. She attended the Kootenai (KOOT-nee) Tribal School, Chemewa Indian School, and Bonners Ferry Public School. Although she contracted tuberculosis during her childhood and required periodic sanitarium treatment, she completed her education, and at only age twenty, served as secretary on the tribal Council.

She married Xavier Aitken in 1954. The couple had six children, but their marriage failed. In 1969, she married David Trice.

For religious reasons, the tribe had resisted moving onto a reservation, but by 1974, the poverty-stricken membership had dwindled to only 67 persons. Trice stated during a media interview that the tribe had nothing at the time, and that there were no jobs available.

Trice was encouraged to run for tribal chairperson. She was elected, and hired Doug Wheaton, her "right hand man," as tribal representative. The two sent letters to the Bureau of Indian Affairs (BIA), but were told that to qualify for housing grants and to rebuild their highway that was in great disrepair, they needed a minimum of 125 tribal members.

Angered, with no other options and on the verge of tribal collapse, Trice decided to declare war—albeit a nonviolent one—on the United States. Most tribes are prohibited under treaty from declaring war on the US Government, but the Kootenai never signed such a treaty. So in 1976, the tribe sold Kootenai Nation War Bonds at one dollar each. The bonds, bearing the signatures of both Trice and Wheaton, contained a brief Declaration of War statement against the United States.

The tribal members' "war" was an implementation of an inventive method popular during the African Americans' 1950s to 1960s fight for social justice: the Kootenai formed informational picket lines at each end of US Highway 95 that runs through Bonners Ferry. They asked politely for a ten-cent toll to drive through what had once been the tribe's ancestral land to help toward care for tribal elders.

After a standoff of several weeks, with neither Trice nor law enforcement officials willing to give in, she led a delegation to Washington, DC. After talks with then-President Gerald Ford, 12.5 acres of federal land were transferred to the tiny tribe for a reservation outside Bonners Ferry; it has now expanded to approximately 4,000 acres.

The action garnered much more attention than the Kootenai expected—not only was it a national news item, it was reported as far away as Israel, Germany, France, and Ireland.

The protest accomplished even more than its goal. In addition to the land they requested, they also gained 18 new houses, a community center, improved water and sewage systems, and in 1996, opened the Kootenai River Casino, which brought in badly needed income.

Also involved in environmental preservation, the tribe operates a hatchery to enable the endangered Kootenai River white sturgeon to recover. The effort became symbolic to the Kootenai, who have seen their own membership increase to 155 persons.

For her accomplishments, Trice was presented the Chairman's Award from the Confederated Salish and Kootenai, and the Women of Color Alliance Breaking Barriers for Women of Color in Idaho Award.

She was a founding member of Upper Columbia United Tribes (UCUT) and other organizations for women's and Native people's welfare.

Trice was a member of St. Ann's Catholic Church and the Altar Society and participated in cultural exchanges with the congregation's non-Native women.

She is also the subject of a documentary by Sonja Rosario, *Idaho's Forgotten War, A Lost Tale of Courage*, which Rosario called, "a testament to what one can do and will do when you love and are committed to your community."

Amelia Cutsack Trice, "The Last War Leader Against the United States," died on July 21, 2011, after an even greater war against cancer. She left a legacy of nonviolent use of the existing system to achieve justice, and is also credited with helping to open doors in leadership for Native American women. As far as is known, Amelia "Amy" Cutsack Trice is the only woman in US history to declare war against the United States Government.

5 LaDonna Harris, Activist

- Received appointments during five US presidential administrations
- Founder, President, Americans for Indian Opportunity

Comanche activist, LaDonna Vita Tabbytite Harris, was born February 15, 1931, in Temple, Oklahoma, to William Crawford, of European descent, and Lilly Tabbytite. When her parents separated shortly after her birth, she was reared in Indian country during the Great Depression by maternal grandparents, John and Wick-kie Tabbytite, on a farm near tiny Walters, Oklahoma.

Her grandfather, part of the last efforts to resist the United States' intrusion on Comanche lands, told stories of those times to young LaDonna. No doubt, they influenced her life course as a Native peoples' advocate.

She married Fred R. Harris, her high school sweetheart, who would become an Oklahoma senator. Now divorced, they have three children, Kathryn, Byron, and Laura. As a senator's wife, she lived in Washington DC during the 1960s, where her high-level contacts extended across the threshold of President Lyndon B. Johnson himself and First Lady, Claudia "Lady Bird" Johnson.

In 1970, Harris founded and serves as president of Americans for Indian Opportunity, a global organization for the economic, political and cultural rights of Indigenous peoples. The organization's website refers to her as "a remarkable statesman and national leader who has enriched the lives of thousands."

She became a member of the short-lived Citizens Party in 1980, was nominated the presidential running mate of Barry Commoner, but was replaced on the Ohio ballot by Wretha Hanson.

Harris has received a number of presidential appointments: Lyndon Johnson chose Harris to serve on the National Council on Indian Opportunity, Richard Nixon selected her for the White House Fellows Commission, and she was appointed by President Ford to the US Commission on the Observance of International Women's Year.

Harris received two appointments under President Carter: special advisor to the Office of Economic Opportunity and as representative of the United States to the United Nations Education, Science and Culture Organization (UNESCO).

In 1994, during the first Clinton administration, Secretary of

Commerce Ron Brown appointed her to the Advisory Council on the National Information Infrastructure.

Harris was instrumental in founding the National Indian Business Association; National Indian Housing Council; and the Council for Energy Resources Tribes. She has served on boards for Save the Children; National Museum of the American Indian; the National Urban League; National Senior Citizens Law Center; and the National Institute for Women of Color.

Besides her work for world peace, women's rights, and the environment, Harris is best known for legislation for the returning of federal recognition to the Menominee Tribe, the introduction of legislation for land return to Native tribes of Alaska, and to the Taos Pueblo Tribe.

She also introduced a program to train Native professionals in utilizing tribal traditional values and outlook in their work, while constructing a global nexus of Indigenous peoples.

In 2000, Harris published her autobiography, *LaDonna Harris: A Comanche Life.*

She is the subject of the documentary film, *LaDonna Harris: Indian 101*, produced and directed by Julianna Brannum. The film reveals Harris' personal struggles that made her a passionate advocate for Indigenous peoples.

EXTRA: AMERICANS FOR INDIAN OPPORTUNITY

The following is the mission statement of Americans for Indian Opportunity as posted on their website:

Americans for Indian Opportunity advances, from an Indigenous worldview, the cultural, political and economic lives of Indigenous peoples in the United States and around the world. Founded by LaDonna Harris (Comanche) and a cohort of her fellow Native American activists in 1970, AIO draws upon traditional Indigenous philosophies to foster value-based leadership, inspire stakeholder-driven solutions, and convene visionary leaders to probe contemporary issues and address challenges of the new century. Governed by a Board of international Indigenous leaders, AIO seeks to create new avenues for international Indigenous interaction, and explore ways Indigenous peoples can influence globalization. AIO is a national nonprofit organization, headquartered in Albuquerque, New Mexico.

---

6 Elouise Pepion Cobell (1945-2011), Native American Rights Advocate, Banker

- Established first national bank owned by a Native American tribe
- Was lead plaintiff in Cobell v. Salazar suit

A great-granddaughter of Mountain Chief, one of the West's legendary leaders, Elouise Cobell (Yellow Bird Woman) was born into the heritage of Blackfeet activism.

She graduated from Great Falls Business College and attended Montana State University. An accountant who was active in community development, Cobell was also involved in many other organizations that benefited Native Indian people.

Cobell never planned to be a banker, but when the town of Browning, Montana, found itself without a bank and people were required to travel 130 miles over rough terrain to Great Falls, Minnesota, Cobell sprang into action. She would start a bank herself, and shoulder all the complications and time investment that such a venture would exact.

Her tenacity paid off when the Blackfeet National Bank opened in 1987 with one million dollars of Blackfeet Tribe capital. It was the first-ever national bank owned by a Native American tribe located on an Indian reservation, and its opening spurred the startup of many other Indian-owned businesses.

Over time, as news spread about the bank's success, Cobell negotiated with eleven other tribes. They purchased the bank and formed the Native American Bank, which became the first ever multi-tribe-owned national bank. By 2007, its ownership included more than two dozen tribes with assets of eighty-six million dollars that encouraged development throughout many Native American communities.

But for all her accomplishments, Cobell is best remembered as the Native American lead plaintiff in the Cobell v Salazar suit filed in June 1996 that challenged the United States' mismanagement of trust funds that belonged to more than 500,000 individual Native American Indians.

According to a 2009 article by Valerie J. Nelson, *Los Angeles Times*, Cobell made a startling discovery during her more than ten years as treasurer of the Blackfeet Confederacy. She found that funds held in trust by the United States Government that were set up as part of the 1887 Dawes Act for both the tribe and individual Indians were mismanaged.

The *Times* article further stated that the Dawes Act issued land to individual American Indians, while holding it in trust and not allowing Native Americans to control their properties. They were to be compensated financially through royalties paid them for grazing, recreational use, and the resources of oil and gas. But the Indians were paid little or nothing.

With the aid of the Intertribal Monitoring Association (of which Cobell was president), she fought for reform for a decade (mid-1980s through mid-1990s). Although she was unsuccessful, she remained undaunted.

Her next step was to solicit help from John Echohawk, executive director of the Native American Rights Fund. He is also recognized by the National Law Journal as one of the 100 most influential lawyers in America. Cobell also teamed with "super lawyer," Keith Harper, and renowned attorney, Thaddeus Holt, whose focus is primarily on litigation and administrative law.

Together, they filed a class-action lawsuit that forced reform and an accounting of the trust funds that belonged to individual Native American Indians.

Under the Obama administration, on December 6, 2010, the government finally negotiated a settlement at $3.4 billion. The major portion was to be used to buy back and restore lands to Native American Tribes. Other portions were used to settle four Indian water-rights cases.

Cobell was bestowed many honors. In 1997, she received a John D. and Catherine T. MacArthur Foundation Genius Grant, for those who "show exceptional merit and promise and for continued and enhanced creative work." She was also awarded an honorary doctorate degree from Montana State University.

In 2002, she received the International Women's Forum Award for Women Who Make a Difference, and the Lannan Foundation Cultural Freedom Fellowship for bringing to light "more than a century of government malfeasance and dishonesty" within the Indian Trust.

Cobell received several additional awards in 2011: an honorary Doctor of Humane Letters from Dartmouth College; the Montana Trial Lawyers Association's Citizens Award; and the Congressional Gold Medal, awarded Cobell in legislation co-sponsored by Senate Majority Leader Harry Reid, Nevada, a Democrat.

A woman for the ages, Elouise Cobell faced and overcame many unique challenges for the betterment of Native American Indian people.

WOMEN OF ALL RED NATIONS (WARN)

- Published exposé on nuclear mining and storage on Indian lands

The most recognized of Native American Indian Women's groups, Women of All Red Nations, held its inaugural conference in Rapid City, South Dakota, in 1974. Many of WARN's members had been active in the American Indian Movement (AIM), co-founded in 1968 by Dennis Banks, George Mitchell, and the sole female, Mary Jane Wilson, an Anishinabe activist. WARN members hailed from 30 different tribal communities and had over 300 members.

Following the arrest of AIM's male leaders, WARN took advantage of their "media invisibility" to champion a number of causes. Among them was the restoration and securing of treaty rights, nuclear mining and storage on Indian lands and adoption of Indian children by non-Indians.

Their citing of involuntary sterilization of Indian women in certain public service hospitals drew attention to such practices and resulted in the United States Department of Health and Human Services issuing regulations governing sterilizations in 1979.

In the 1990s WARN expanded their interests to include interacting with other women's groups and advocating for Indian men, with special focus on those within the prison population.

7 LORELEI DECORA (WINNEBAGO)

- WARN Co-Founder

In 1973 at age nineteen, Lorelei DeCora participated in the Wounded Knee siege to protest lesser standards of justice for Native American Indians. In 1974, she was cleared in federal court and all charges against her were dismissed.

But the siege at Wounded Knee had awakened in her a desire that would direct her life's path. As inexperienced DeCora acted as medic and tended those with gunshot and other wounds, she realized the great need for healthcare providers in her Native American community of Porcupine.

As one of nine districts of the Pine Ridge (South Dakota) Reservation, it is part of Shannon County, the third poorest in the nation according to the latest US Census Bureau statistics.

DeCora returned to school, earned a bachelor's degree in nursing from South Dakota State University (1986), and spearheaded the building of a badly needed Indian health clinic on the Pine Ridge Reservation.

As she noticed the many cases of diabetes and related illnesses, in 1993 DeCora instituted Diabetes Wellness: American Indian Talking Circles at Pine Ridge and three other reservations to address the pandemic through self-education and prevention.

In the same year, she was awarded a $100,000 Robert Wood

Johnson Foundation Community Health Leader stipend to further fund the Porcupine Clinic and expand her vision that included trained Indian healthcare providers. It gained her national recognition.

Since 1996 DeCora has worked full-time in the Talking Circles project and formed what she calls "a wellness coalition" with the Porcupine Clinic.

Lorelei DeCora's vision for community-centered healthcare and self-education to prevent disease is a continuation of her lifetime activism on behalf of her community.

8 MADONNA THUNDERHAWK (TWO KETTLE LAKOTA)

In 2005, Madonna Thunderhawk was principal organizer of the Lakota People's Law Project (LPLP) and is its tribal liaison. The organization states on its website that the current focus is its fight for the return of more than 2,000 Lakota children that have been illegally removed from their homes by state authorities and placed in non-Indian foster care homes.

Thunderhawk, who states her life goal as, "winning justice for American Indians and renewing Native American culture in the United States," has participated in every modern Native American Indian struggle.

She was a founder and spokesperson for the Black Hills Alliance (1970s) to prevent Union Carbide and other companies from uranium mining on land the Lakota deem sacred, and is an original member and spokesperson of the American Indian Movement (AIM, organized in Minneapolis in 1968).

Thunderhawk participated in the occupation of Alcatraz Island (November 20, 1969 to June 11, 1971) and the 71-day Wounded Knee siege in February 1973.

But she also fashions regalia for powwow dancers. She designed costumes for the TNT movie, *Crazy Horse*, and was featured in the PBS documentary series, *We Shall Remain*.

9 PHYLLIS YOUNG
(OGLALA LAKOTA)

She was the only woman of four Lakota representatives who delivered a letter of "Lakotah" secession from the United States to the US Department of State on December 17, 2007. The action followed years of discussions among the Lakota. The group, each member a participant in the 1973 Wounded Knee siege, accused the government of gross treaty violations.

Young continues to speak for the rights of the Lakota people.

10 JANET MCCLOUD
(TULALIP/NISQUALLY, 1934–2003)

Dubbed the "Rosa Parks of the American Indian Movement," during the 1960s and 1970s, Janet McCloud (Yet-Si-Blue) published a newsletter that documented her people's struggle regarding tribal fishing rights. It presented the Native American Indian's viewpoint on what some termed "the fish wars."

In the 1854 Treaty of Medicine Creek, the federal government guaranteed the Nisqually, Puyallup, and others named in the treaty hunting rights in their tribal lands and waters. Yet, state agents harassed Native Americans for exercising their rights, charged them with infractions including "operating set nets capable of taking game fish," and placed them under arrest.

McCloud helped to stage "fish-ins" that asserted tribal treaty rights, but violated state laws. Her actions eventually led to the 1964 Boldt Decision, which restored Indians' fishing rights in the Nisqually and Puyallup rivers.

She joined the American Indian Movement (AIM) in the early 1970s, and later in the decade, co-founded WARN and also worked to end domestic violence in Indian communities.

11 ALBERTA SCHENCK (OR SKENK, 1928-2009), ESKIMO CIVIL RIGHTS PROTESTER

- "Alaska's Rosa Parks"

Alberta Daisy Schenck was born in Nome, Alaska, to Albert Schenck, a Euro-American Army veteran of World War I, and Mary Pushruk-Schenck, of Native Inupiat heritage.

As a high school girl in 1944, Alberta's class had been studying about the Constitution, the United States Civil War, and President Abraham Lincoln's freeing of the slaves. It made her think of similar unequal treatment of her Eskimo people by Euro-Americans.

She was employed as an usher at the Dreamland Theater, but her sole duty was to make sure that Native Eskimo people did not sit on the "white" side, even if the Eskimo side were filled, and seats were available on the other side.

The rule made no sense to Alberta. It also turned other Eskimos against her. When she complained about the restrictions to the manager, she was fired.

In an action that would put into motion a series of occurrences that would earn her the belated title, "Alaska's Rosa Parks," Alberta telephoned the Nome office of an army major. At her request, he agreed to meet her for lunch.

As they sat across from each other at the Nome Grill that noon, she handed him a theme she had written for class that explained her viewpoint. It was a logical appeal for justice and equality for the Eskimo people.

Wasn't it their land before the Euro-American people arrived? And yet, their presence and their rules had instilled a sense of inferiority in the Eskimo. The newcomers had overlooked Eskimo contributions to the Red Cross drive, the fact that they enlisted in the military—as her own brother had done—and supported the bond drives.

The major encouraged her to take her theme to the *Nome*

Nugget newspaper. It appeared in the next issue as a "Letter to the Editor" under her signature.

It caused quite a stir. The wife of a local store manager wrote a response in protest that appeared in the following issue. Alberta delivered a second response, but the "hot button" subject was over with, as far as the editor of the *Nugget* was concerned.

The issue, however, continued to simmer among the Nome population, even as life proceeded as usual until a United States sergeant, a Euro-American newly stationed in Nome, invited Alberta to the movies … and to sit with him on the "white" side.

Management was called. The police came, ejected her from the theater, and jailed her for her "infraction."

But the zeitgeist moment had come, and Alberta was the perfect vessel to initiate change: her aunt, Frances Longley, was a member of the Arctic Native Sisterhood in Nome, and as such, had direct connections to Roy Peratrovich, who was grand president of the Alaska Native Brotherhood. His wife, Elizabeth, was equally supportive in battling discrimination against Alaskan Natives.

The group of civil rights advocates had the added advantage of close ties to Territorial Senator O. D. Cochran, his children, and Alaska's governor, Ernest Gruening. Better still, the flashpoint of Alberta's treatment at the theater had also stirred the Eskimo masses to action.

The following Sunday, in a coordinated effort, great numbers of them bought tickets, stormed into the theater and sat wherever they pleased.

Details of the incident were wired to Governor Ernest Gruening in Juneau. He demanded from the mayor a full and complete investigation, and to report back to him immediately. In a matter of hours, the mayor wired a response to the governor: "A mistake has been made. It won't happen again."

The major who had encouraged Alberta had stated previously regarding the Eskimo: "Many have served creditably in various theaters during the recent war … They have seen the outside world. Theoretical democracy has been a part of their indoctrination.

Can they be expected to return to their native villages to resume again a position of dumb acceptance of the white man's word or wish as the law of their village?"

It was Alberta's courage, and the crucial testimony of Elizabeth Peratrovich, that stirred the collective conscience and contributed to the passage of the Alaska Anti-Discrimination Bill.

In 2011, Alberta Schenck was inducted into the Alaska Women's Hall of Fame.

The 2009 movie, *For the Rights of All: Ending Jim Crow in Alaska*," profiles the struggle for Alaska Natives' equal rights.

---

12 Dahteste, Warrior

- Was mediator between the US military and the Apache

Information about her, including the dates of her birth and death, is sketchy, but Dahteste (ta-DOT-say)was a member of the Chiricahua Band, she fought with Geronimo during the Apache wars against Mexico for having slaughtered Geronimo's family, and against the United States for its encroachment and colonization of Apache ancestral lands. Married and a mother, Dahteste was reputed to have been very beautiful, fastidious about her appearance, and yet, chose the warrior's path.

Dahteste was celebrated for her warrior skills and participated in raiding parties and battles alongside her husband and their family friend, Geronimo.

A trusted scout and messenger, Dahteste also spoke fluent English, was a mediator between the US military and the Apache, and helped to convince the band to give up the fight when surrender remained their only viable option. Even so, the US military sent her to prison along with the other survivors of Geronimo's resistance Band.

Dahteste (unlike untold numbers of other Native American Indians) survived both pneumonia and tuberculosis during her eight years in a squalid Florida prison. Along with Geronimo and others, she was eventually transferred to prison at Fort Sill,

Oklahoma, as Apache prisoners of war.

After nineteen years, Dahteste was allowed to return to her home, where she lived to a great age on the Mescalero Apache Reservation.

Extra: Geronimo!

The yell, "Geronimo!" is attributed to a US paratrooper, Private Aubrey Eberhardt, during WW II. It was inspired by the 1939 movie, *Geronimo* (with Preston Foster, Ellen Drew, Andy Devine, and Chief Thundercloud).

When Eberhardt yelled, "Geronimo!" he initiated it to shore up courage when parachuting from airplanes, and a shout honoring a Native American that would forever indicate bravery was born.

The Apache warrior's Chiricahua name, Goyathlay, however, meant "one who yawns." The name Geronimo was given him by Mexican soldiers.

Perhaps one of the least known facts about him is that toward the end of his life, Geronimo accepted the Christian faith, and on July 1, 1903, was baptized in Medicine Creek, Oklahoma Territory. The following is excerpted from his own words:

"I am not ashamed to be a Christian, and I am glad to know that the President of the United States is a Christian, for without the help of the Almighty I do not think he could rightly judge in ruling so many people. I have advised all of my people who are not Christians, to study that religion, because it seems to me the best religion in enabling one to live right."

With S. M. Barrett as recorder and editor, he published his own book, *Geronimo's Story of His Life* (1906).

A version of this article, Osama Bin Laden, Geronimo and the Native American Perspective appeared as a blog by KB Schaller, Christianpost.com/bindings, July 8, 2011.

13 ZITKALA-SHA (GERTRUDE SIMMONS BONNIN, 1876-1938), ACTIVIST

- Author, Musician, Educator
- Co-composed the first Native American Opera

Gertrude Bonnin's Dakota/Sioux name, Zitkala-Sha, means "red bird," but missionaries gave her the name, Gertrude. She was born on the Pine Ridge, South Dakota Reservation and reared by her mother, Ellen Simmons, a full-blooded Sioux. Her father was a Euro-American who abandoned the family while she was very young.

When she was eight years old, missionaries took Bonnin and several other Native Indian children to White's Manual Labor Training Institute, founded by Josiah White, a Quaker, to educate poor children regardless of race. Bonnin attended for three years. Later, in *The School Days of an Indian Girl*, she wrote of the elation she felt in learning to read, write, and play the violin. But she also described the pain of having all of her Native heritage stripped away.

When she returned to the reservation at age eleven, she found that she did not fit fully into either culture. At age fifteen, she returned to the training institute, but this time with the mindset to master the violin and piano. Her success in both qualified her to replace the music teacher when she resigned.

When Bonnin received her diploma in 1895, she delivered a speech on women's inequality. It was a trendy subject at the time and garnered her accolades from the local newspaper.

She did not return to the reservation after her graduation, but with the scholarship she received, enrolled at Earlham College in Richmond, Indiana.

Bonnin later took a position as music teacher at Carlisle Indian Industrial School in Pennsylvania, founded by Colonel Richard Henry Pratt, whose ambition and philosophy were to "kill the Indian, save the man."

While there, Bonnin played violin with the Boston Conservatory of Music and in 1900, as a member of the Carlisle Indian Band, traveled with the group to play at the Paris Exposition.

In the same year, she wrote articles on Native American life that were published in the prestigious periodicals, *Atlantic Monthly* and *Harper's Monthly*.

When Pratt sent Bonnin back to the reservation to recruit additional students, while there, she observed Euro-American settlers occupying lands promised to the Yankton Dakota through the 1887 Dawes Act. As she became more aware of injustices against Native Indian people, when she returned to Carlisle, she criticized the school's rigid programs to assimilate Indian children into Euro-American culture and questioned an education that prepared them for only manual or domestic careers.

In 1901, Bonnin published another article in *Harper's* that described the alienation and loss of identity Native children suffered at Carlisle. Pratt, already under fire by some for abuse and exploitation of students' labor in spite of receiving funds to educate them, apparently did not appreciate such criticism of his leadership. Soon after Bonnin's article was published, she was dismissed from her teaching position.

Bonnin was commissioned by Ginn and Company in the same year to gather stories from reservation Indians for her book, *Old Indian Legends*.

She took a job as clerk at the Bureau of Indian Affairs (1902), where she met and married Captain Raymond Bonnin, a mixed-heritage Nakota. When he was reassigned, the couple moved to the Uintah and Ouray Reservation in Utah. Homeland of the Ute Tribe, it is second only in land area to the Navajo.

For fourteen years, Bonnin taught there for the Indian Service. She gave birth to their only child, a son, Ohiya (Winner), and also met William Hanson, a Brigham Young University professor and composer.

It was there in 1910 that she collaborated with him on music for the Native American opera, "Sundance." Bonnin wrote the libretto and songs, and in 1913, the reservation's Utes performed the first opera co-authored by a Native American.

Bonnin loved music, but felt a stronger obligation to fight for Native Indian rights through her writings and political activism. She and Captain Bonnin joined the Society of American Indians and, in 1916, she was elected the group's secretary.

In 1924 with two Euro-American co-authors, Bonnin wrote *Oklahoma's Poor Rich Indians: An Orgy of Graft, Exploitation of the Five Civilized Tribes, Legalized Robbery*. Not only did it expose thefts and even murders of Native Americans, it led to the 1934 Indian Reorganization Act that reestablished a trust for Indian Lands.

Through organizing pan-Indian unity for political power, Bonnin was also a strong voice in gaining citizenship and voting rights (1924) for Native Americans. Furthermore, in 1926 the National Council of American Indians was established out of these efforts. She served as its president for the remainder of her life.

Among Bonnin's other writings are *Impressions of an Indian Childhood*, *Old Indian Legends*, and *American Indian Stories*.

---

14 PRINCESS ANGELINE
(CA. 1820-1896)

- Refused to move
- Credited with saving Seattle's residents from a massacre

The eldest daughter of the great Chief Seattle (whose Catholic baptismal name was Noah Seattle) had several names in the Lushootseed language: Kikisoblu, Kick-is-om-lo, and Wewick. Born in what is now Rainier Beach in Seattle, Washington, she was given the name Angeline by early Euro-American settlers and the title, "Princess," was conferred upon her because of her lineage.

When the 1855 Treaty of Point Elliott demanded all Duwamish Indians be relocated from their homelands to reservations to allow for Euro-American progress, Angeline remained in her waterfront cabin near present day Pike Place Market. She did laundry and sold hand-woven baskets through Ye Olde Curiosity Shoppe to support herself.

Princess Angeline became world-famous and was frequently seen seated on the sidewalk reciting her beads. She is also credited with saving Seattle's residents from a massacre. Because of her ancestry and character, Princess Angeline was a notable figure and a friend of many of Seattle's early settlers.

According to the chronicle of Holy Names Academy, she was the last direct descendent of Chief Seattle for whom their city was named. In her later years, gnarled and wrinkled, she walked slowly and painfully with the aid of a cane, wore a signature red handkerchief on her head, and a shawl about her shoulders.

When Princess Angeline died, the Seattle community showed kindness toward the woman who, for many years, had been a visible link to its Native American Indian past.

They extended compassion toward the daughter of Chief Seattle and provided a magnificent funeral in the Church of Our Lady of Good Help.

Her casket was formed in the shape of a canoe, and she was buried in Lake View Cemetery on Capitol Hill.

For the first time in nearly one hundred years, two art works that represent her—an oil painting on canvas and a plaster bust—are on exhibit at Seattle's Museum of History and Industry.

South Angeline Street in Seattle is one of the sites named in her honor.

15 Nancy Ward (ca. 1738-1822 or 1824), Warrior, Diplomat

- De facto ambassador between the Cherokee and Euro-Americans

In the Cherokee society of her day, Nancy Ward (Nanyehi, One who goes about), as a Ghigau—Beloved Woman of the Cherokee

Nation—was allowed to sit in councils, make decisions, and grant pardons. She believed that the Cherokee should live peaceably with the Euro-Americans.

According to Nancy Ward's page on the SmithDRays website, she was born in Chota, de facto capital of the Cherokee Nation and was a member of the Wolf Clan.

At age fourteen, Nancy married Tsu-la (Kingfisher) and gave birth to a daughter and a son.

During the Battle of Taliwa against the Creeks (1755), she fought at her husband's side. When Tsu-la was killed, she took up his rifle and led her people to victory. It earned her the title, War Woman, and later, Ghigau.

She married again, this time Bryant Ward, a South Carolina colonist and trader and gave birth to a second daughter, Elizabeth (Betsy) Ward.

During the Revolutionary War, Nancy Ward's cousin, Dragging Canoe, and his supporters planned attacks on area whites. She sent messengers to warn them ahead of time. For her deed, she was named "Patriot for the Daughters of the American Revolution" and also of the "Society of the Sons of the American Revolution."

In 1776, the Cherokee attacked the Fort Watauga settlement on the Watauga River and took a Euro-American woman, Lydia Russell Bean, captive. Nancy used her power as ghigau to spare her life. She also took Bean into her own home and cared for her wounds. Upon recovery, she taught Ward a new weaving technique that revolutionized the way the Cherokee made garments. With two of her own dairy cows that she rescued from the settlement, Bean also taught Ward to raise cattle, churn butter, and make cheese—skills that helped to sustain the Cherokee during the times when wild game was scarce.

Through Bean's actions and Ward's willingness to learn new skills, the Cherokee evolved from a communal agrarian society into one that resembled that of their European counterparts. But as the need for labor grew, Ward also became the first Cherokee slave owner.

When the sale of Cherokee lands to Euro-Americans became an issue, Ward and other members of the Women's Council raised objections, but were largely ignored. In 1781, as the de facto ambassador between the Cherokee and Euro-Americans, Ward met with the American delegation to discuss their settlements along the Little Pigeon River. It was further proof of the high regard in which her people held her. In 1819 when the Cherokee enacted a Constitution, she supported it.

An important figure in Cherokee history, her actions, tribal status, and the respect in which she was regarded by both the Cherokee and the Euro-Americans also made her an early example of women's voices in American politics.

Extra: Clans of the Cherokee

There are seven clans of the Cherokee: Wolf, Bird, Deer, Long Hair, Blue, Wild Potato, and Red Paint.

Members are considered as brothers and sisters and may not marry within their clans. Because the society is matrilineal, clan membership is attained through the mother, and women are the traditional heads of households.

---

16 Kalyn Free, Attorney-at-Law

- First woman ever elected District Attorney for Pittsburg and Haskell Counties
- Named one of the Top Fifty Women in Oklahoma

Attorney and member of the Choctaw Nation of Oklahoma, Kalyn Free, in 2005 founded and was president of the Indigenous Democratic Network, known throughout Indian country as INDN's List. It was the only political organization that recruited, trained, and funded American Indian candidates and staff and mobilized the Indian vote throughout America.

With the help of INDN's List, forty-five tribal members were elected (and re-elected) since 2006 and now serve in state and local offices across the United States. Free states that she is most proud to have helped elect the first Indian woman to the Washington

State Senate and to statewide office in Montana.

Herself politically active, Kalyn Free ran for the United States Congress in 2004 with the support and endorsement of 117 Indian tribes, AFL-CIO, EMILY's List, Sierra Club, 21st century Democrats, and Democracy for America. She served as a Super Delegate on the Democratic National Committee (2005-2009).

While INDN's list was a functioning entity, Free devoted her time and energy to the organization and the INDN's List Education Fund. But in spite of all its successes, the Indigenous Democratic Network was forced to shut its doors in January 2011 due to funding issues.

As an attorney, her experience in state and federal courtrooms, coupled with her vast knowledge of governmental agencies and the political scene, uniquely qualify her to assist tribal governments and individuals in addressing complex environmental and legal issues.

Free has been active in public service in Washington DC; Oklahoma, her home state; and nationally for twenty-five years. After she graduated from law school, Free was the youngest lawyer ever hired by the United States Department of Justice (DOJ).

During her ten years with DOJ, she served as senior counsel in the Indian Resources Section where she supervised environmental litigation throughout Indian country. Her two most notable cases were the filing of the first joint complaint between the United States and Indian Nations in history. It involved the Puyallup and Muckleshoot in Washington State, and the first Safe Drinking Water Act case for pollution of drinking water on the Sac and Fox Reservation in Oklahoma.

After leaving DOJ, Free returned to southeastern Oklahoma and became the first woman elected district attorney (DA) of Pittsburg and Haskell counties. During her tenure, she made victims' rights, domestic violence, and child abuse priorities in her administration.

She increased significantly the prosecution of domestic violence and child abuse cases, while racking up record-setting verdicts in the courtroom. Free has successfully prosecuted first-degree murderers, pedophiles, wife-killers, rapists, drug dealers, and dozens of corporate polluters.

Kalyn Free focuses her practice on legal issues important to Native American Indians, with a special emphasis on prosecution of corporate polluters who pollute Indian country.

For six years, Free served as lead counsel for the Ponca Tribe against a Taiwanese corporation in the largest class action ever certified in an environmental case in Indian country. The case settled in 2009 for $10.6 million.

In 2003, she obtained a settlement for a single individual for more than one million dollars against a natural gas company for polluting his pond.

She has received numerous awards recognizing her dedication to fighting for those who have no other voice, including the Arthur S. Fleming Award for Outstanding Service to the federal government; the American Bar Association's Spirit of Excellence Award for her efforts to increase minority hiring at the US Department of Justice; the Oklahoma Institute of Child Advocacy's Friend of Children Award; and the Oklahoma Coalition Against Domestic Violence and Sexual Assault's Make a Difference Award.

She also received the 21st century Democrats 2006 Rising Star Award, and the National Education Association's 2007 Leo Reano Memorial Award for her inspiring work with American Indians.

Kalyn Free has also contributed opinion pieces in publications on her experiences as a Native American woman:

http://books.google.com/books?id=bgvwzP9QwhYC&q=kalyn+fre e#v= twopage&q=kalyn%20free&f=true

Her husband, Steve Bruner, served on the Muscogee National Council until 2012, when he chose not to seek re-election. She considers Wegas and Ofi, her "children," and says, "Each has four paws, and are German shepherds."

EXTRA: INDIAN'S LIST

According to its mission statement, the vision of INDN's List was to build a country where diversity is celebrated, civil rights are never negotiable, and where the equal rights and opportunities for all people that were promised in the Constitution over two centuries ago would be fully realized.

"My dream lives on of seeing the first Indian woman in Congress, an Indian governor, and ultimately an Indian president. They are all out there, somewhere. And maybe, just maybe, INDN's List has helped show them the way," she states.

Kalyn Free further believes that when Native American Indian children and adults witness other Indians running for and winning higher offices, future generations will be inspired to cast their vote to make the Indian voice a palpable force in American politics.

II.

SINGERS, MUSICIANS AND DANCERS

NATIVE AMERICAN WOMEN HAVE LONG PARTICIpated in varieties of dance, from tribal to classical ballet. They are also innovative as songwriters, composers, musicians and vocalists.

17 MARY YOUNGBLOOD (B. 1958), FLUTIST, COMPOSER, SINGER

- First Native American to win two Grammy Awards

Born in Sacramento, California, and reared as Mary Edwards by adoptive parents, Dr. Bob and Leah Edwards, Mary Youngblood (Aleut/Seminole), was only age four when she began to pick out melodies on the piano. At age five, she started formal lessons, and at age six, held her first piano recital.

A member of her high school concert, pep, and marching bands, she learned classical flute and also mastered the guitar, synthesizer, piano, slit drum, and marimba. She honed her singing voice in church choirs and played folk rock in bar bands.

In time, however, like many adopted children, Mary became curious to find her biological parents, but did not meet her birth mother, Nadine Matsen, until she was twenty-six years old. The experience changed her life. She immersed herself in her birth culture and took her biological father's surname.

For ten years, Youngblood worked in sales of high-end Native American art and crafts and was on the Board of Directors for the Sacramento Urban Indian Health Project.

It was not until her early 30s that she took interest in the Native flute; it would launch her to fame. Because of her training in classical flute, in only a matter of days, she had mastered the instrument and played her first engagement only one month later.

Even though in most Native American Indian communities the reed flute is played only by men, Youngblood defied tradition. Her big break came when her music, on audio cassette, was given away as a gift for donations during the PBS fundraising special, *American Indian Circles of Wisdom*. She shopped around copies of the cassette and eventually signed with Silver Wave independent music.

Soon afterward, she was dubbed, "First Lady of the Flute," and the country's premiere Native American musician. She has received three Native American Music Awards and was the first woman to win Flutist of the Year (1999, 2000). She was named Best Female Artist (2000) and became the first Native American person to win two Grammy Awards: *Beneath the Raven Moon* and *Dance with the Wind* (2002, 2006).

Her solo album, *Sacred Place: A Mary Youngblood Collection* (2008) is said to "take the artistry of Native American flute music to its highest level."

Grammy nominated *Heart of the World* fuses guitar, dulcimer, cittern, the eagle bone whistle, and drums with vocals by Joanne Shenandoah. Proceeds from each sale help to support the U'wa people of the rainforest, who call their South American homeland, "Heart of the World," in their struggle against global oil companies that threaten their lands.

In 2007, Youngblood composed and played *Spirit of Sacagawea* with Jim Brock. Narrated by actress Tantoo Cardinal, it was nominated for the Musical Score EMMY Award.

Other Grammy nominations include *Feed the Fire* (2004) and *The Offering* (both 1999).

She is author of two instructional books on the reed flute and has planned an instructional video.

Extra: The Youngblood Signature Flute

The newest Mary Youngblood Signature Flute was introduced at the Potomac Festival in March 2013. Made of Alaskan yellow cedar and crafted according to Mary's exact specifications by Randy and Shelly Stenzel, it is in the key of A minor. Each flute comes with a certificate of authenticity signed by Mary.

For more information, visit:

http://www.featherridgeflutes.com/Signature_Flute_Page_1.html

---

The Five Moons
Internationally famous
Oklahoma prima ballerinas

During the 20th century, five accomplished Native American ballerinas rose to international prominence, each from the state of Oklahoma. Bronze statues in their honor were dubbed, *The Five Moons*. Larger than life, they are displayed in the garden of the Tulsa Historical society.

When Oklahoma celebrated its powerful dance heritage on October 8, 1997, Governor Frank Keating designated the five Native American ballerinas, "Oklahoma Treasures." The ceremony took place at the state capitol and was a fusion of classical and tribal styles.

All five of the women were born when government statutes prohibited all tribal rituals, so powwows and other ceremonies were held in secret in order to keep Native cultures alive. Each of the ballerinas recalled the excitement they felt as children when they participated in these secret gatherings.

As they sat on the podium, ceremonial shawls created by members of their respective tribes were presented to each of the dancers to be worn freely at powwows where all were welcome.

18 Maria Tallchief
(Elizabeth Marie Tallchief, 1925-2013)

Celebrated for her musicality, strength, and technical precision, ballet dancer, teacher, and artistic director Maria Tallchief (Osage) was born in Fairfax, Oklahoma.

Her family moved to Los Angeles so that she and her sister, Marjorie, could receive the best ballet training. She joined the Ballet Russe de Monte Carlo in the 1940s.

Tallchief married George Balanchine (1946, separated 1951), a Russian ballet dancer, international choreographer, and founder of the New York City Ballet in 1948. Tallchief joined in the same year. Among her most notable performances are *The Firebird*, *Orpheus*, and *The Nutcracker*.

In 1957 Tallchief married again, this time to Henry Paschen. She gave birth to a daughter. Along with her work with the New York City Ballet, she was a guest performer with the American Ballet Theatre.

After she retired in 1966, she worked with the Lyric Opera Ballet and Chicago City Ballet, which she co-founded. For her contributions to the arts, Maria Tallchief was awarded the Kennedy Center Honors, also in 1966.

19 Marjorie Louise Tallchief
(b. 1926)

Maria Tallchief's younger sister, Marjorie (Osage), was born in Denver, Colorado, but grew up in Fairfax, Oklahoma, along with her sister, Maria, and brother, Gerald. The family moved to Los Angeles to further the girls' ballet training.

The first Native American premiere *danseuse étoile* in the Paris Opera, she danced with the American *Ballet Russe de Monte Carlo* (1946-1947); the *Grand Ballet du Marquis de Cuevas* (1948-1955) and other companies.

Among her most acclaimed performances were *Night Shadow* (1950), *Romeo and Juliet*, and *Giselle* (1955, 1957).

Tallchief was director of dance for Civic Ballet Academy, Dallas, Texas; City Ballet in Chicago; and the Harid Conservatory, Boca Raton, Florida (1989), where she remained until her retirement in 1993.

She danced for heads state that included John F. Kennedy, Charles de Gaulle, and Lyndon B. Johnson.

Marjorie Tallchief was inducted into the Oklahoma Hall of Fame in 1991. In May 1992, the University of Oklahoma presented her a Distinguished Service award.

20 Rosella Hightower
(1920-2008)

Ballerina, teacher, and director, Rosella Hightower, Choctaw descent, was born in Durwood, Oklahoma. She was the only child of Charles Edgar Hightower and Eula May Flanning Hightower. The family moved to Kansas City, Kansas, when Rosella was five. She began ballet training with a local instructor at age thirteen and later studied in New York.

In 1938, Hightower began her dancing career at the *Ballet Russe de Monte Carlo* and performed with several other companies, including the American Ballet Theatre.

Hightower was made *Chevalier de la Legion d'Honneur*, France's premier honor (1975) and, in 1981, became the first American to direct the *Ballet de l'Opera National de Paris*.

21 YVONNE CHOUTEAU (MYRA YVONNE CHOUTEAU, B. 1929)

A member of the Shawnee Tribe, Yvonne Chouteau grew up in Vinita, Oklahoma. At age fourteen, she became the youngest dancer ever to be accepted by the *Ballet Russe de Monte Carlo*. Her first solo role was as "Prayer" in *Coppelia* (1945).

She and husband, Miguel Terekhov, organized the Oklahoma City Civic Ballet (now Oklahoma City Ballet), and in 1962 founded the School of Dance at the University of Oklahoma. It is the nation's first fully accredited university dance program. At age eighteen, Chouteau became the youngest member ever to be inducted into the Oklahoma Hall of Fame.

22 MOSCELYNE LARKIN (EDNA MOSCELYNE LARKIN, 1925-2012)

The daughter of a Peoria/Shawnee father and a mother who was a Russian ballerina, Moscelyne Larkin was born in Miami, Oklahoma. Her mother was her ballet teacher until she moved to New York to continue her training.

At age fifteen, Larkin joined the Original Ballet Russe and danced for the *Ballet Russe de Monte Carlo*.

She married Romans Jansinsky and the two moved to Tulsa, Oklahoma, where they founded the Tulsa Ballet Theatre.

In 1978, Larkin was inducted into the Oklahoma Hall of Fame. Other honors include the annual *Dance Magazine* Award in 1988. She was inducted into the Oklahoma Women's Hall of Fame (1993) and also named Outstanding Indian by the Council of American Indians.

EXTRA: TRIBUTE TO THE MOONS

The Four Moons ballet was created for the 1967 Oklahoma Indian Ballerina Festival and set to music by composer,

Louis Ballard, an Oklahoma Quapaw-Cherokee, to honor the ballerinas.

In consideration of the shared heritage of the Tallchief sisters, four solos honored the dancers' tribal heritage.

Chickasaw artist, Mike Larsen, created a mural, *Flight of Spirit*, which depicted each dancer in a signature pose. It formed the backdrop for the ceremony and hangs in the Oklahoma State Capitol rotunda in Oklahoma City.

A painting, *The Four Moons*, by Muscogee Creek artist, Jerome Tiger, graced the cover of the ballet program. Lili Cockerille Livingston wrote a biography of the women titled, *American Indian Ballerinas*. Moscelyne Larkin, however, requested not to be included.

The Five Moons sculpture was begun by Monte England in 1995. When he died in 2005 before completing it, his friend and fellow sculptor, Gary Henson, completed the project, which also depicted each ballerina in a signature pose. It was unveiled at the Tulsa Historical Society in November 2007.

EXTRA: THE THUNDERBIRD AMERICAN INDIAN DANCERS

The Thunderbird American Indian Dancers was founded in 1963 by American Indian men and women who were native New Yorkers. The troupe is the oldest resident Native American dance company in New York.

Its founders were descendants of Hopi, Mohawk, San Blas, and Winnebago, all "first-generation" New Yorkers, whose parents had been born on reservations. It was organized to preserve traditions, songs, and dances they had learned from their parents.

Housed in the old McBurney YMCA facility, within a few years, the troupe took to the road, adding to its repertoire from other Native American Indians as they performed on reservations throughout the continental USA. Its dancers have won powwow contests where standards are extremely high.

Louis Mofsie (Hopi/Winnebago), one of the founders, now age seventy-six and an accomplished dancer in his own right, is the group's choreographer and artistic director.

Other founders include his late sister, Josephine Mofsie; Muriel Miguel (Cuna/Rapahannock); Rosemary Richmond (Mohawk); and Jack Preston (Seneca, deceased).

The company receives no government or corporate support. Along with its dedication to cultural awareness, the troupe's proceeds support Native scholars through The Thunderbird American Indian Dancers Scholarship Fund.

23 Amber Rose Cleveland and the Fancy Shawl Dance

- 2012 Competition Winner, Gathering of the Nations

When 24-year-old (Ho-Chunk/Nakoda) Amber Rose Cleveland— First Place award winner in the Women's Fancy Shawl Competition at the 2012 annual Gathering of Nations—danced, it was amid a spectacle of color and movement: fringed shawls, beaded over-lay tops, flared skirts over moccasins and leggings, and flashes of beaded earrings and neck-drop chokers. Precise footwork moved to the rhythms of song and drumbeat.

According to Autumn Whitefield-Madrano in an *Indian Country Today* article, the Women's Fancy Shawl Dance is a fairly recent arrival on the powwow dance scene and is an offshoot of men's dances created in the 1920s and extending into the 1930s, an era when the United States and Canadian governments banned all American Indian religious dances.

Some say it was men of the Ponca Tribe who innovated the Men's Fancy Dance to avoid disobeying the government mandate while presenting a colorful spectacle non-Indian audiences would pay to see.

First called the Graceful Shawl Dance, the Women's Fancy Shawl is an off-shoot from the men's dances. It was well-known by the 1940s, declined in the 1950s and is a departure from the generations-old women's dances of regality and restraint.

During the 1960s and 1970s, an era of tribal reawakening and activism, Fancy Shawl experienced a revival and progressed to more athletic and innovative. While the dance requires stamina and grace, modesty and restraint are still strong expectations during jumps and spins.

Watch Amber Rose Cleveland on YouTube as she competes at the Red Lake Independence Day Powwow, 2010.

24 Lisa Odjig, World Champion Hoop Dancer

- First adult female World Champion Hoop Dancer

In the once males-only competition, Lisa Odjig made history when she became the first adult female to win the Hoop Dance World Championship. Not once, but twice (2000, 2003).

Although she has not competed since 2007, more recently, she displayed her skills in the *Canada's Got Talent* competition and gained national exposure. She competed against thirty-five other contestants and advanced to the semi-final round. The televised show, a counterpart to *America's Got Talent*, allows anyone or any group to showcase their talents before judges and a live audience.

Although Odjig advanced to the final round, she felt her loss may have been because *Canada's Got Talent* added dancers and drummers to her routine that she had not expected, which threw her routine off.

Her appearance in the national spotlight, however, has stirred wider interest in Native American dance. Festivals and other organizations have expressed interest in having Odjig perform the complicated dance that involves perfect rhythmic timing, while arranging sometimes a dozen or more hoops in patterns that include animals and other images.

In addition to being a two-time winner of the annual hoop

dancing championship held in Phoenix each year, she has been a four-time runner-up and has also won seven other US and Canadian competitions.

A program associate for Toronto's Harbourfront Centre, she explains her absence from competitions for the past years on seeking to balance work with time to practice her already amazing hoop dancing skills.

Watch Lisa perform the hoop dance on YouTube:

http://www.youtube.com/watch?v=oUOQV0EbUXk

EXTRA: HOOP DANCE TRIVIA

According to Wikipedia, in 1994, Jackie Bird (Mandan/ Hidatsa/Santee Sioux) from South Dakota was the first woman to compete in the Hoop Dance World Championships.

Ginger Sykes (Navajo) from Arizona was the first woman to win the Championship, when she was awarded First Place in the Teen Division.

When Jasmine Pickner (Lakota) performed at Mount Rushmore in 2009, she was featured in the PBS documentary, *The National Parks: America's Best Idea.*

---

25 SHARON EAGLEMAN, EDUCATION RESEARCH ANALYST

- Champion Jingle Dress dancer
- Addressed significance of women's roles within the powwow circle

According to the University of Idaho News website, Sharon Eagleman's talk at its Native American Student Center and Women's Center in April 2011 would explain the role of women within the powwow circle. Eagleman would also explain how the roles go beyond the powwow to influence her everyday life, career, family, and education.

A championship Jingle Dress dancer, she has spent much of her life traveling the "powwow circuit." In an interview with Steve

Martin, Native American Student Center Director, she further explains the importance of the powwow as also a social event where friends and family get together.

The enrolled member of the Ft. Peck Sioux Assiniboine/Little Traverse Band of Ottawa also explained why Native American dances are important to non-natives as well as Native Americans as a reminder that they are still part of Indian culture. They may be performed during naming ceremonies and other rites, including graduations and leaving home for the military.

But for Eagleman, it is not only about the dance. She is an education research analyst at Haskell Indian Nations University. She holds a bachelor of arts degree in psychology from Montana State University-Billings, and a master of education degree in educational leadership from North Dakota State University.

For approximately a decade, she has worked with American Indian Students in higher education in student affairs to support and assist them toward success.

Sharon Eagleman's interview, "In Other Words with Sharon Eagleman and Steve Martin," may be viewed on YouTube.

Extra: The Jingle Dress Dance

The Jingle Dress Dance may be performed in the traditional or contemporary style. The dress itself is fashioned from cloth, with several rows of metal cones sewn across the skirt, and sometimes the blouse.

In the traditional Jingle Dress, footwork is light, danced close to the ground and performed in a pattern. The dancer never crosses her feet, does not perform a complete circle, or dance backward.

The contemporary dance, by contrast, may be fancier and the dress may be designed to accommodate the dancer's footwork. Also, the dancer may cross her feet, turn full circles, and dance backward.

26 Mildred Rinker Bailey (1907-1951), Jazz Singer

- Paved the way for jazz greats

Born to Josephine (Coeur d'Alene [Schitsu'umsh]) and Charles Rinker in Tekoa, Washington, Mildred Rinker was reared on the reservation in a musical family. Her father played fiddle and called square dances; her mother, a devout Catholic, played piano and taught Mildred to play and sing.

Her brothers were also musicians. While Alton (Al) plied his talents on the professional vaudeville circuit (as Al Rinker), Charles was a lyricist.

When the family moved to Seattle in 1913, Mildred and her brothers befriended a fellow Washingtonian, Harry Lillis "Bing" Crosby. By age seventeen, while living with relatives, Mildred worked at Woolworth's demonstrating sheet music. She honed her singing and speaking talents on radio shows and performing in clubs.

Her first marriage to Ted Bailey, a salesman, ended in divorce, but she kept Ted's last name as a career choice. She thought it sounded more "American" than Rinker.

She married again, and with her second husband, Benny Stafford, moved to Los Angeles, where her career took off in nightclubs on Sunset Strip.

In 1925, both Bing Crosby and Al Rinker dropped out of college and drove from Spokane to Hollywood where Mildred introduced them to her best show business contacts. By 1926, Crosby and Al Rinker (both were working for society bandleader Paul Whiteman) teamed with Harry Barris in a nationally acclaimed trio, The Rhythm Boys.

To repay Mildred for helping them to get started, in 1929 Crosby introduced her to Whiteman. Known as "the King of Jazz," he hired her immediately.

Her debut rendition of *Moaning Low* was an immediate hit on his popular radio show and by 1930, Mildred was his highest paid performer. Even so, she did not begin to record with Whiteman until late 1931. She was a popular performer, but left in 1932 because of a salary dispute.

Bailey recorded with several other companies and performed with the Dorsey Brothers as her accompanists. She worked with Benny Goodman in an all-star session that featured Coleman Hawkins, one of the 20th century's most important jazz figures and the first major saxophonist in the history of jazz.

But Bailey's second marriage also ended, and in the mid-1930s she married Kenneth "Red" Norvo, one of jazz's early vibraphonists. A trendy couple, they were dubbed "Mr. and Mrs. Swing." Even so, in 1942, her third marriage ended in divorce as well, but they continued to record together until 1945.

Among Bailey's most notable recordings are *I'd Love to Take Orders from You* and *Honeysuckle Rose*, both in 1935; *Rockin' Chair* (1937) was so popular it earned her the name, "The Rockin' Chair Lady."

With Norvo, she had two No. 1 songs: *Please Be Kind* and *Says My Heart* (1939). *Darn That Dream* (1940) was recorded by Benny Goodman and His Orchestra.

She did not advertise her Indian heritage and accounts of the day described her as "white," but her Coeur d'Alene people have reclaimed her.

In 1989, Mildred Rinker Bailey was inducted into the Big Band and Jazz Hall of Fame, but her tribe introduced a resolution in the Idaho Legislature. They hope it will convince Jazz at Lincoln Center in New York City to add her to its inductees as a pioneer who blazed a trail for female greats such as Ella Fitzgerald and Billie Holliday.

27 Buffy Sainte-Marie (b. 1941), Singer, Musician, Activist

- Academy Award Winner, Best Music, Original Song

Buffy (born Beverly) Sainte-Marie, is a Canadian Cree who is probably best known as a protest singer-songwriter and composer who has mastered percussion, mouthbow, ukulele, autoharp, and harmonica. In addition, she is a self-taught guitarist, pianist, and visual artist.

A pacifist, educator, and social activist as well, Sainte-Marie was born on the Piapot Reserve, Craven, Saskatchewan, Canada. Orphaned, she was adopted by relatives, Albert and Winifred Sainte-Marie, and grew up in Wakefield, Massachusetts.

Sainte-Marie earned her BA degree (1963) and PhD (1983) from the University of Massachusetts Amherst in teaching and Oriental philosophy and graduated in the top ten of her class.

In 1964, she returned to the Cree Reserve and was adopted by Imu Piapot (youngest son of Chief Piapot) and his wife. As she learned about a heritage she knew little about, she became established in her culture.

Her career budded in college with songs that included *Now That the Buffalo's Gone*, and while still in her early 20s, toured alone as she honed her performing skills at folk music festivals on Native American Indian Reservations across the United States, Canada, and abroad.

She released her debut album *It's My Way* (Vanguard Records, 1964) for which *Billboard* magazine named her Best New Artist, and also in 1964, released *My Country 'T'is of Thy People You're Dying*, which was considered controversial and incendiary at the time because it addressed issues that Native Americans faced.

Her album, *Coincidence and Likely Stories* (1992) featured *The Big Ones Get Away* and *Bury My Heart at Wounded Knee*, also considered incendiary because they, too, mentioned the plight of Native Americans, and in addition, Leonard Peltier, imprisoned former AIM leader who many still believe to be a political prisoner.

As she became more popular, artists including Janis Joplin, Chet Atkins, and Taj Mahal began to perform many of her earlier songs, which climbed to the top of the charts.

In 1963, Sainte-Marie wrote *Universal Soldier* as a tribute to veterans who returned wounded from Viet Nam.

In the late 1960s, she moved to Hawaii where she met and married surfing instructor, Dewain Bugbee of Hawaii. The union ended in 1972.

She married Sheldon Peters Wolfchild, an actor, in 1975. She gave birth to a son, Dakota "Cody" Starblanket Wolfchild, and from 1976 to 1981, took an absence from the music scene. During this time, she appeared with her young son on *Sesame Street* in order to teach children that Indians still existed.

After her marriage to Wolfchild also ended in divorce, she married again (1983), this time, to veteran producer Jack Nitzche (who died in 2000).

Also an actress, in the movie, *Son of the Morning Star* (1991), Sainte-Marie was the voice of Kate Bighead, the Cheyenne character through whom the Native American side of the Battle of the Little Bighorn (that resulted in the death of Lieutenant Colonel George Custer) was told.

In 1992, she portrayed an Iroquois clan mother/matriarch in the television film, *The Broken Chain*, in which two Mohawk friends recount the 1700s face-off between the French and the Iroquois Confederacy.

She won an Academy Award in 1983 for *Up Where We Belong* (music by Jack Nitzche and Sainte-Marie; lyrics by Will Jennings), from the movie, *An Officer and a Gentleman*. It also won her both Golden Globe and BAFTA film Awards for Best Original Song, and received a Canadian Gemini Award for her variety special by the same name in 1996.

Sainte-Marie has exhibited works at the Winnipeg Art Gallery; Glenbow Museum (Calgary); American Indian Arts Museum (Santa Fe); and the Emily Carr Gallery (Vancouver).

In 2002 she sang at the Kennedy Space Center for Commander John Herrington (Chickasaw), USN, the first Native American astronaut, and in 2003, was a spokesperson for UNESCO Associated Schools Project Network (Canada). She holds a number of honorary doctorate degrees from universities all across Canada.

She released *Buffy/Changing Woman/Sweet America: The Mid-1970s* (2008). In the same year, she made a comeback in Canada when she released *Running for the Drum*, and in 2010 received the Governor General's Performing Arts Award.

Buffy Sainte-Marie's career has always focused on issues that affect Indigenous peoples.

---

28 RADMILLA CODY

- Miss Navajo Nation 1997-1998
- Grammy Awards nominee
- Native American Music Awards, Best Female Artist
- Advocate for victims of domestic violence

Born on the rural Navajo Reservation, Radmilla Cody was reared by her Navajo maternal grandmother, Dorothy, who taught her to speak the Navajo language, but discouraged her from speaking English, although Radmilla became fluent in both.

She states on her website that she had always wanted to be a singer. But, because Radmilla was required to herd sheep as part of her daily chores, she spent long hours alone where she practiced her singing—with sheep as her first audience.

While she loved Whitney Houston and Diana Ross in her childhood, she was also influenced by the Navajo songs her medicine man grandfather sang as he rode his horse. Because Grandmother Dorothy was a Christian convert, Radmilla also visited the local church and was influenced by their choirs.

When time came for the 1997 Miss Navajo competition, one of the requirements was fluency in the Navajo Language, an ability more strongly stressed than those of Western models of beauty pageants, which focus on physical appearance.

A model of striking beauty, Radmilla decided to enter the pageant. She excelled in all the required areas and was awarded the title of Miss Navajo (Nation). But, because she is of both Navajo and African American racial heritage, her selection was not without controversy. Through her Navajo mother, Margaret, however, she learned to embrace both sides of her heritage. After her Miss Navajo reign, she began to focus on her career as a recording artist, singing both traditional songs and others that are composed by her uncle, Herman Cody.

In 2002, she won the Native American Music Award for Best Female Artist. In the same year, she honored John Herrington (the first enrolled member of a Native American tribe to fly into space) by singing the Navajo version of the Star Spangled Banner at the Kennedy Space Center.

Despite her successes, in 2003 her life took a downward turn for a time and resulted in her incarceration for several months. After regaining her freedom, Cody became an activist against domestic and teen dating violence.

Turning adversity into a positive, Cody has earned a public relations degree, and is working toward a graduate degree in sociology while continuing her music, which she calls, "my medicine."

Her recordings include *Within the Four Directions* (2000); *Seed of Life* (2002) for which she won a Native American Music Awards Best Female Artist; *Spirit of a Woman* (2005); *Precious Friends* (2007); and *Shi Keyah: Songs for the People* (2011).

Nominated in three categories for the 2013 Native American Music Awards—Traditional Album, Record of the Year, and Best Female Artist—Radmilla Cody garnered the Record of the Year Award for *Shi Keyah, Songs for the People.*

For more Information about her music, visit the Official Homepage of Radmilla Cody.

III.
STORYTELLERS, AUTHORS AND POETS

NATIVE AMERICAN TRADITIONS ARE RICH IN STO-
rytelling. In times past, Indigenous peoples relied on their elders
to entertain and pass down their history, customs and legends to
the younger generation.

The oral traditions are still strong elements, but many stories
are now written down to further preserve them for generations
to come.

29 MOURNING DOVE (CHRISTINE QUINTASKET, B. CA. 1888-1936), AUTHOR

- First published Native American novelist

Christine (or Christal) Quintasket was born around 1888 to
Joseph Quintasket (Okanagan), and Lucy Stukin, of Colville
ancestry. Her Indian name was Humishuma (a close Okanagan
translation for Mourning Dove).

According to family lore, Christine was born in a canoe on
the Kootenai River near Bonner's Ferry, Idaho, and was then
wrapped in a steersman's shirt. She spent most of her life on the
Colville Reservation in Washington State. Her heritage language
was Salish, and she spent her early years with a number of sisters

and brothers near Kettle Falls. Each summer, she took part in the great salmon fishery.

Quintasket learned traditional life ways and other teachings from her grandmother and an older woman whom the family had apparently taken in. It was an adopted Euro-American orphan, who was also part of their household, however, who taught her to read.

When he used dime novels to teach Quintasket to read, Therese Broderick's *The Brand: A Tale of the Flathead Reservation* placed in Quintasket the burning desire to become a novelist also.

In 1894 when she entered the Goodwin Catholic Mission School near Kettle Falls, she spoke of being punished for speaking Salish (it was the practice of schools of the times to prohibit Native American Indian children from speaking or practicing their languages or customs). When the school closed in 1900, Quintasket transferred to the Fort Spokane agency.

After her mother died in 1902, Christine managed the household until her father remarried (1904) and then transferred to the Fort Shaw Indian Boarding School (famous for its World Championship girls basketball team) near Great Falls, Montana.

She married Hector McLeod (1909) of the Flathead Nation, but when their marriage became troubled, they separated. Around 1912 when Quintasket was living alone in Portland, Oregon, her dream resurfaced to become a novelist. Her idea was to interweave buffalo roundups that she witnessed in Montana and traditional tribal life within an exciting love story.

It was also during this period that Quintasket realized she would have to improve her writing skills to achieve her dream of becoming a novelist. It was also then that she began to refer to herself as Humishuma, and made her way to the Calgary College business school, where she studied typing, composition, bookkeeping, and shorthand.

By 1915, she had produced a draft of *Co-Ge-Wea, the Half-Blood: A Depiction of the Great Montana Cattle Range*. The tale of the "half breed" caught between two cultures was a popular theme of the time, but her story was a departure from most, one of few with a woman—a Native American Indian woman—as its central character.

At an annual Frontier Day festival in Walla Walla, Washington, she met tribal advocate and founder of American Archaeologist, Lucullus McWhorter who encouraged Quintasket—Mourning Dove—to tell her peoples' stories. The two would correspond for more than twenty years.

Mourning Dove did much of her writing after working up to ten hours daily picking fruit in Washington State orchards. She also taught at Inkameep Day School (1917-1919) and began to gather and record Okanagan traditional stories in order to preserve them for posterity.

When her novel, *Co-Ge-Wea, the Half-Blood*, was finally published (1927), she was surprised to see a heavily-edited final version with the editor's viewpoint interwoven throughout. She expressed her astonishment, but did not complain.

Her next book, *Coyote Stories* (1933), met with the same heavy editing that eliminated Native American customs and anything else the editor felt Euro-American readers would find offensive. Even though the foreword was by Chief Standing Bear himself, the Colville-Okanagan elders did not recognize the stories as they had originally told them.

In 1971, Donald Hines re-edited some of the Okanagan folklore that Mourning Dove had collected, and in 1981 released a new edition of *Cogewea: The Half-Blood*. In 1990, her miscellaneous writings were organized into *Mourning Dove: A Salishan Autobiography*.

More than a novelist and ethnographer, however, Mourning Dove also strove to dispel many unfounded mainstream myths and perceptions of Native American Indians, either as the "Noble Savage" or as ruthless murderers. In a 1916 interview with a Spokane newspaper, she commented on the Euro-American stereotype of the Native American Indian:

"It is all wrong, the saying that Indians do not feel as deeply as whites. We do feel, and by-and-by some of us are going to be able to make our feelings appreciated, and then will the true Indian character be revealed."

During the latter years of her life, she became more and more involved with the Bureau of Indian Affairs in carrying out its "Fair Deal for Indians," and also became the first woman elected to the Colville Tribal Council (1935).

Her political and cultural achievements for the betterment of the Okanagan are now cherished not only by her people, but studied and appreciated worldwide.

30 Sarah Winnemucca (ca. 1844-1871), Author, Activist

- First Native American to obtain a United States Copyright

Her Paiute name, Thocmentony, means Shell Flower. She was born in the Humboldt Lake area of what is now western Nevada. Her father, Old Winnemucca, was leader of a small Northern Paiute band. Her grandfather, Tru-Ki-Zo (or Truckee), believed in peaceful coexistence with the Euro-Americans and was a guide for John C. Fremont in his exploration of the Great Basin and California. Tru-Ki-Zo's assistance earned him many friendships.

When Sarah was around ten years old, Tru-Ki-Zo called on those contacts to obtain a Euro-American education for her and her sister, Elma. Along with their mother, he took the girls, who were reared in the Paiute tradition, to the Sacramento area in California, where Sarah learned Spanish and began to pick up English.

When she was later placed in the home of Major William Ormsby in Carson City, Nevada, she and Elma became companions to his daughter. The friendship enabled Sara to become fluent in English. Before long, she became one of very few Nevada Paiutes able to read and write English.

In accordance with his wishes, sometime between 1858 to 1861, Sarah and Elma were enrolled in school at the Convent of Notre Dame (San Jose) run by the Sisters of Charity, but withdrew because of Euro-American objections to their attendance. Sarah worked for a time as a domestic while continuing her education on her own.

In 1861 Tru-Ki-Zo, who had been such an influence in her life, died. By 1871, because Sarah had developed proficient language skills, she worked as an interpreter for the Bureau of Indian Affairs at Fort McDermitt (Oregon). She served United States troops as both interpreter and scout and rendered service in the 1878 Bannock War. Her responsibilities, however, incurred distrust in her people.

In time, as Euro-American lust grew for more land, in spite of her service to the military, Winnemucca and her people were sent to a series of reservations: Pyramid Lake in Nevada, the Malheur in Oregon, and lastly, to Yakima, Washington.

Even as she endured their rejection, Winnemucca remained an advocate for her people. When she published *Life Among the Paiutes, Their Wrongs and Claims* (1883), she became the first Native American in history to obtain a United States copyright.

She was liaison between the army and the Paiutes, interpreter and teacher at the Yakima Reservation where the army detained Paiute prisoners, and criticized Indian agents and missionaries for their mistreatment of Paiutes. She traveled to Washington to plead for Paiute causes and gave hundreds of lectures that attacked bad government policies, corrupt Indian agents, and insensitive missionaries.

While visiting in Boston, she met pioneer kindergarten educator, Elizabeth Palmer Peabody, and her sister, Mary Tyler Mann (widow of Horace Mann, who had a major impact on educational reform throughout America). With their support and encouragement, Winnemucca built a school in Nevada that promoted Indian language and lifestyle, but shortly afterward, was forced to close when Native American Indian children were required to attend English-speaking boarding schools.

In 1994 more than a century later, Sarah Winnemucca was finally recognized for her skills, service to the United States, and loyalty to her people. A Washoe County school was named in her honor, and in 2005, her statue was added to the National Statuary Hall in the United States Capitol.

31 Joy Harjo (b. 1951) Poet, Educator, Musician

- Called "one of America's foremost Native voices"
- Named "Writer of the Year for Film Scripts"

Enrolled member of the Muskogee Tribe Joy Harjo was born in Tulsa, Oklahoma. She attended the Institute of American Indian Arts in New Mexico, where she studied theater and painting. She earned her BA degree from the University of New Mexico in 1976 and her MFA degree from the University of Iowa.

At a time when the mood of Indian America called for speakers and singers to articulate its temper, beliefs, and dreams, Joy Harjo conveyed them through her poems and songs. Having mastered the saxophone, she combined its music with her works, along with combinations of tribal music, rock, and jazz.

Called by critics, "one of America's foremost Native voices," Harjo taught at the Institute of American Indian Arts (1978-79), was a lecturer at Arizona State University (1980-1981), and also taught at Santa Fe Community College (1983-84).

She studied filmmaking in a non-degree program at the Anthropology Film Center and has taught at universities in Arizona, New Mexico, and California. She was a full professor at the University of New Mexico (1991-1995) and currently teaches at the University of California at Los Angeles.

In 2005, Harjo was named Writer of the Year for Film Scripts by the Wordcraft Circle of Native Writers and Storytellers, for *A Thousand Roads*, created for the National Museum of the American Indian.

Her works have been published in magazines including *River Styx*; *Ploughshares*; *Massachusetts Review*; and in the *Pushcart Prize Poetry Anthologies XIII and XV*.

Among her many other honors, Joy Harjo was named one of the Outstanding Young Women in America (1978, 1984) and won first place in poetry in the Santa Fe Festival of the Arts (1980).

Her 1990 poetry collection *In Mad Love and War* won an American Book Award and the Delmore Schwartz Memorial Award, while *The Woman Who Fell from the Sky* (1994) won the Oklahoma Book Award.

She was named Writer of the Year-Poetry (2003-2004) for *How We Became Human: New and Selected Poems 1975-2001*, and Storyteller of the Year for her CD, *Native Joy for Real*, also in 2003-2004. Her celebrated works also include *She Had Some Horses* (1983), *In Mad Love and War* (1990), and *The Last Song* (1975).

Among other affiliations, she is a member of the PEN New Mexico Advisory Board and held past membership in the Native American Public Broadcasting Consortium Board of Directors (1987-1990).

---

32 Leslie Marmon Silko (b. 1948), Author, Educator, Poet

- Named one of "Four Native American Literary Masters"

One of the key figures in what contemporary Native American studies scholar, Kenneth Lincoln, has called the Native American Renaissance, Leslie Marmon Silko (Laguna Pueblo/multi-racial) was born in Albuquerque, New Mexico, to Leland Howard Marmon and Mary Virginia Leslie.

She attended Laguna Day school through fifth grade, graduated from a Catholic grade school in Albuquerque, and received her bachelor's degree from the University of New Mexico (1969). She married Richard C. Chapman (1966; divorced, 1969). They had one son, Robert William Chapman.

While still in school, her short story, *The Man to Send Rain Clouds* (1967), published in *New Mexico Quarterly*, brought her notice in the literary world as a new and sterling Native American voice and earned her a grant from the National Endowment for the Humanities. The book continues to be included in today's anthologies.

In 1969, she entered law school at the University of New Mexico under the American Indian Law School Fellowship Program, and married John Silko (they, too, would later divorce). Choosing instead to employ storytelling as a means to foster justice for her people, Silko left law school in 1971 to teach on the Navajo Reservation at Tsaile, Arizona.

She published more short stories and many poems from 1968 through 1974. In 1972, she gave birth to a second son, Cazimir, and in 1978, moved to Tucson, where she began teaching at the University of Arizona.

Silko's novel, *Ceremony* (1977, 1986), earned rave reviews and remains the single Native American novel that continues to appear on college and university syllabi. Other titles include *Almanac of the Dead* (1991) and *Gardens in the Dunes* (2000).

Her poetry and short story collections include *Laguna Women: Poems* (1974); *Storyteller* (1981); *Sacred Water: Narratives and Pictures* (1994); *Rain* (1996) and *The Turquoise Ledge: A Memoir* (2010).

Among her numerous awards and recognitions are the National Endowment for the Arts' Discovery Grant (1971); the Pushcart Prize for Poetry (1977); and New Mexico Endowment for the Humanities' Living Cultural Treasures award (1988).

With the *Delicacy and Strength of Lace: Letters Between Leslie Marmon Silko and James Wright* (1986) won her the Boston Globe prize for non-fiction.

For her short story, *Lullaby*, Silko was also the youngest writer ever to be included in *The Norton Anthology of Women's Literature*.

Along with Pulitzer Prize winner, N. Scott Momaday (Kiowa descent), Gerald Vizenor (Anishinaabe), and James Welch (Blackfeet/Gros Ventre), Silko has been included by author, and David Ross Boyd Professor of English, Alan R. Velie, as one of his "Four Native American Literary Masters."

33 KAREN LOUISE ERDRICH (B.1954), AUTHOR

- Winner, 2012 National Book Award for Fiction
- Finalist, 2009 Pulitzer Prize

Turtle Mountain Band of Chippewa Indians member, Karen Louise Erdrich (more widely known as Louise Erdrich), was born in Little Falls, Minnesota, to a Chippewa mother and a German-American father.

A novelist, short story writer, and poet, she has been called by critic, Kenneth Lincoln, one of the most significant writers of the second wave of what he terms the "Native American Renaissance."

The eldest of seven siblings, Erdrich grew up in Wahpeton, North Dakota, where both parents taught at the Bureau of Indian Affairs.

In 1972 as a Dartmouth College freshman in the year that the Native American Studies department was created, she met Michael Dorris (Modoc/French/Irish), an anthropologist and chairman of the department.

She earned a bachelor's degree at Dartmouth (1976) and a master's degree in creative writing from Johns Hopkins University (1979).

Erdrich wrote short stories and many poems during this period, and in 1978, began to correspond with Dorris on writing projects while he was in New Zealand.

The two married in 1981, the year Erdrich gathered materials that would comprise *Jacklight* (1984), a poetry collection that was primarily an outgrowth of her master's thesis.

She and Michael Dorris had six children, three of them adopted while Dorris was still single and three biological daughters.

Erdrich won the $5,000 Nelson Algren Prize for Short Fiction for her short story, *The World's Greatest Fisherman* (1982). She later expanded it to become the first chapter of her debut novel, *Love Medicine*, which won the 1984 National Book Critics Circle Award. It launched her as a *New York Times* bestselling author, and brought her critical acclaim and attention in the literary world.

Erdrich and Dorris collaborated into the 1990s, but as their lives and the marriage became increasingly more troubled, the couple separated. Dorris died in 1997 by his own hand.

But Erdrich's works would continue to garner praise. *The Plague of Doves* (2008) was a 2009 finalist for the Pulitzer Prize in Fiction. *The Round House*, which describes a young man's revenge for the rape of his mother in a Native American community won a 2012 Best Book Award for Fiction, and a 2013 Rough Rider Award—the state of North Dakota's highest honor.

Erdrich has also written non-fiction: *The Blue Jay's Dance: A Birth Year* (1995) and *Books and Islands in Ojibwe Country* (2003). She has authored story collections and children's literature. Other poetry collections are *Baptism of Desire* (1989), and *Original Fire: Selected and New Poems* (2003).

Her prestigious awards and recognitions also include the O. Henry Award for her short story, "Fleur" (*Esquire*, August, 1986, 1987), and a Guggenheim Fellowship, among many others.

Karen Louise Erdrich owns Birchbark Books, an independent bookstore that specializes in Native American literature and focuses on the Twin Cities' Native American Indian community.

EXTRA: THE ROUGH RIDER AWARD

According to the North Dakota Office of the Governor website: An honorary rank of colonel in the North Dakota Theodore Roosevelt Rough Riders was established during the 1961 Dakota Territory Centennial. The award recognizes present or former North Dakotans who have been influenced by this state in achieving national recognition in their fields of endeavor, thereby reflecting credit and honor upon North Dakota and its citizens.

Recipients of the award are chosen by the governor, with the concurrence of the Secretary of State, and the director of the State Historical Society.

As of April 2013, thirty-nine North Dakotans have received the award. Their portraits are on display in the lower level of the capitol building, including the latest recipient, Louise Erdrich.

Erdrich is only the third author to be conferred a Rough Rider Award. Louis L'Amour (1972) and Larry Woiwode (1992) were previous winners.

34 DIANE GLANCY (1941), PLAYWRIGHT, POET, MOVIE DIRECTOR

"The ordinary life I write about is from the harshness, the fullness of this land."

—Diane Glancy,
from her award-winning autobiographical work,
Claiming Breath (1992)

Diane Glancy was born Helen Diane Hall in Kansas City, Missouri, to Lewis Hall (Cherokee) and Edith Wood Hall (English and German descent). She attended schools in Kansas City, Indianapolis and, also, Saint Louis where she graduated from Normandy High School (1959).

She received her bachelor's degree from the University of Missouri (1964). In the same year, she married Dwane Glancy and the couple moved to Tulsa, Oklahoma. They had two children, David and Jennifer. She completed her master's degree at Central State University (Edmond, Oklahoma 1983) and worked as artist-in-residence for the State Arts Council of Oklahoma.

After her children graduated from high school, Erdrich applied for, and was accepted by the Iowa Writers Workshop in Iowa City where she earned her MFA degree (1988).

She accepted a position at Macalester College (Saint Paul, 1989), taught Native American literature and creative writing, and is now its professor emeritus. She was Visiting Richard Thomas Professor of Creative Writing at Kenyon College in Gambier, Ohio (2008-2009), and was appointed Distinguished Professor at Azusa Pacific University (2012).

Glancy's writings cover a wide range. Her poetry includes *Iron Woman*, which won the Capricorn Poetry Prize (1990). In *Lone*

Dog's Winter Count, winner of a Minnesota Book Award (1991), Glancy uses poems as verbal pictographs—voices of the past and present—to describe events in her life.

Trigger Dance (1990) was her first collection of short fiction and won the Mildren P. Nilon Award for Minority Fiction.

Her novels include: *The Reason for Crows* (2009), a story of Kateri Tekakwitha, a 17th century Mohawk maiden converted by the Jesuits (canonized by the Catholic Church in 2012) and *Pushing the Bear: After the Trail of Tears* (2009), sequel to *Pushing the Bear: a Novel of the 1838-1839 Cherokee Trail of Tears* (1996).

She has also written and directed short films: *Ride Between the Worlds* and *On the Shore of Their Country*.

In 2010, she wrote and co-directed her feature-length film, *The Dome of Heaven*, which featured acclaimed Native actor, Wes Studi. It won Best Native American Film at the Trail Dance Festival (2011).

The *Words of My Roaring* (2006) is one of her many plays. In 2013, Native Voices at the Autry produced *The Bird House*. Set in the back room of a fading Texas church, the play explores the lives of an aging pastor and his two sisters as each adjusts to the uncertainties of what lies ahead for them.

Her nonfiction includes *Freeing the First Amendment: Critical Perspectives on Freedom of Expression* (1995) and *Naming Myself: Writings on Identity* (1995).

Glancy has received a National Museum of the American Indian Expressive Arts Grant; a Pushcart Prize; two National Endowment for the Arts fellowships; and a Sundance Screenwriting Fellowship, among many other awards.

A preview of *The Dome of Heaven*, written by Diane Glancy, directed by Diane Glancy and Jeremy Osbern, can be viewed on YouTube.

IV.
ATTORNEYS, LEADERS AND POLITICIANS

MORE AND MORE, NATIVE AMERICAN WOMEN ARE venturing into non-traditional arenas of leadership.

---

35 ANGELIQUE EAGLEWOMAN (B. 1970), LAW PROFESSOR

- Built program that focuses on Native American Law

Professor Angelique EagleWoman (Sisseton-Wahpeton Oyate), in an interview by Associated Press writer Jessie L. Bonner, decided early on that justice would be her pursuit.

It was in 1978 at only age eight that EagleWoman's uncle, an African-American who had married into her family, was beaten by five deputies when he went to pay a speeding ticket. The court awarded him $75,000 in punitive damages.

Now a James E. Rogers Fellow in American Indian Law at the University of Idaho College of Law, EagleWoman has made good her vow and has built a program that focuses on Native American law.

A complicated specialty, it is frequently misinterpreted, mis-comprehended, and sometimes ignored. Since the 1970s, only a few attorneys with the expertise have been available to guide tribal members through complex legal matters that are made even more daunting given tribal governments' frequently understaffed legal offices.

In a speech at the University of San Diego in February 2011, however, EagleWoman not only condensed the entire overview of tribal law and US Federal Indian Law into an hour-and-a-half presentation, her lecture also included the origins of US Federal Indian law jurisprudence.

She covered the Marshall Trilogy—three 1800s Supreme Court decisions regarding American Indians that were presided over by Chief Justice John Marshall, which helped to establish present federal Indian law.

Discussions included complex tribal jurisdiction laws and restrictions that make the handling of violent crimes on Tribal lands problematic. EagleWoman also included Indian gaming under the Indian Gaming Regulatory Act.

To conclude her presentation, EagleWoman discussed the Declaration on the Rights of Indigenous Peoples, which, although it originated in 1982, was not adopted by the United Nations until 2007.

Among other guarantees, it established individual and collective rights of Indigenous peoples in several areas: culture, language, health, education, identity, and employment.

---

36 Betty Mae Tiger Jumper (1922-2011) Tribal Leader, Author

- First and only female chairperson, Seminole Tribe of Florida, Inc.
- Inducted by governor into Florida Women's Hall of Fame

Born in Indiantown, Florida to a Seminole mother and a Euro-American father on April 27, 1922, Betty Mae Tiger Jumper's life was destined to be marked by the extraordinary.

Because Seminole children of Euro-American heritage were believed to bring "bad luck" to the tribe, traditional law of the time demanded they be put to death, and all of the prescribed methods were equally gruesome for those such as Betty Mae and her two-year-old brother, Howard: strangulation, abandonment in the woods, drowning, or having their mouths stuffed with mud.

When the medicine men decided that it was time that the law be carried out, they came to their great-uncle Jimmie Gopher's home. But their Uncle Jimmie had abandoned such beliefs when he became a Christian and would not hear of it. He ordered them off his property at gunpoint. Later, he moved the children to the Dania/Hollywood (Florida) community, where Betty Mae and Howard would be safe.

Ironically, in years to come, the same young girl whose life Seminole law had demanded, would amass a resume replete with "firsts" that benefited her people.

She attended the Cherokee Indian School in North Carolina, and in 1949 became the first Seminole to earn a high school diploma. Jumper was the Seminole's first public health nurse, its first health director, and first to institute the Indian Health Program to foster improved health care for her tribe.

In 1957, she served on the first council that helped to organize Florida Seminole government, which enabled her people to obtain federal recognition. She was also elected to the tribe's board of directors.

As Jumper continued to demonstrate exceptional skills, she was elected as the tribe's first—and to date its only—female chairperson. She served from 1967 to 1971. She is also believed to be the first woman elected as chairperson or chief of any federally recognized tribe.

Through financial savvy, Jumper brought the Seminole Tribe—which had less than forty dollars in its treasury when she took office—to a surplus of a half-million dollars by the end of her tenure. Other programs she instituted include the leasing of Seminole lands to outside businesses, which brought in additional revenues.

She founded *Smoke Signals*, the tribe's first newspaper (1963) and was its editor for many years. It was renamed *Alligator Times* in 1973 and in 1982, became the colorful, award-winning *Seminole Tribune*. Also a columnist for the newspaper, she shared colorful snippets and historical anecdotes of Seminole life.

While Jumper was chairperson, the United Southeastern Tribes (USET) was formed in 1968 to bring together the Seminole, Miccosukee, Cherokee, and Choctaw. It grew to become one of the most powerful lobbies in Indian country. The coalition has since expanded to include more than two dozen additional tribes that share the responsibilities of directing educational and health concerns for its membership.

In 1970, Jumper was one of two women appointed by President Nixon to the National Congress on Indian Opportunity. In 1994, Governor Lawton Chiles inducted her into the Florida Women's Hall of Fame. In the same year, Florida State University conferred on her an honorary doctor of humane letters degree for her many years of commitment to improving the education, health, cultural and economic conditions of her people. The honor made Jumper the first Native American to receive such a distinction from the university.

Dr. Betty Mae Tiger Jumper was instrumental in establishing Chickee Independent Baptist Church on the Seminole Indian Reservation. It was so named because it began beneath a chickee—an open-sided thatched-roof dwelling supported by upright cypress logs—to serve the tribe's Christian community.

She was also instrumental in the erecting of the present church building, which exists close to where the original chickee stood. She and other elders taught youngsters to sing hymns and songs in the Creek and Mikasuki languages to help to preserve them.

Dr. Jumper was author of *And With the Wagon Came the Word* (2000), which chronicled the introduction of the Christian faith to the Seminole people and also wrote *Seminole Legends* in 1998.

Each story was beautifully illustrated with a full-color original painting by artist and friend-to the-Seminoles, Guy LaBree, to preserve ancient tribal stories for younger generations.

---

37 WILMA MANKILLER (1945-2010), ACTIVIST, POLITICAL LEADER

- First female principal chief of Cherokee Nation
- Awarded Presidential Medal of Freedom

Born in Tahlequah, Oklahoma, Wilma Pearl Mankiller was the sixth of eleven children born to Charley Mankiller (Cherokee) and Clara Irene Sitton (Dutch/Irish heritage). The Mankillers lived in extreme poverty.

In 1956 under the Bureau of Indian Affairs' Indian Relocation program, the family moved willingly to San Francisco, where Wilma became involved in the Indian Center, but the family continued to struggle in their new home because of racial discrimination and declining finances.

At age seventeen, she married Hector Hugo Olaya de Bardi, an Ecuadorian college student. They moved to Oakland, and after the birth of daughters Felicia and Gina, Mankiller returned to Skyline Community College in San Mateo (California) County. She also attended San Francisco State University for a time.

Mankiller became politically active in the 1960s, and an advocate for American Indian people. For five years, she was a volunteer to the then-poverty stricken Pit River Tribe.

She joined Indians of All Tribes (IAT) when 80 to 90 of them, mostly Indian college students, occupied Alcatraz Island to demand "the return of Alcatraz to Native American Indians and sufficient funding to build, maintain, and operate an Indian cultural complex and a university."

Further purposes of the occupation included drawing attention to Indian problems and beginning an Indian movement.

The US Government rejected all their demands and the

protest, which lasted from November 20, 1969 to June 11, 1971, ended after the tide of public support turned against IAT and US government forces moved in and forcibly removed the few who remained.

Hector and Wilma would divorce in 1977, and she would return with her daughters to Oklahoma. She began work for the Cherokee Nation's government as a tribal planner and program developer. She enrolled at Flaming Rainbow University in Stilwell, and earned her bachelor's degree in the social sciences. She would later take graduate courses at the University of Arkansas.

After Principal Chief Ross Swimmer resigned in 1985 to head the Bureau of Indian Affairs, Mankiller became the first female principal chief of the Cherokee Nation. She married again in 1986, this time to Charlie Soap, and in 1987, she was elected to a term in her own right. Mankiller was reelected in 1991, but did not seek another term in 1995, due to health issues.

During her administration, she improved her nation's health care, education system, and infrastructure. A hydroelectric facility was built and tribally-owned businesses established. She also improved the relationship between the US Federal Government and the Cherokee Nation.

Even so, her administration was not without controversy. Among them was that Mankiller limited Cherokee citizenship by establishing a law that excluded the Freedmen (descendents of slaves owned by the Cherokee) section of Cherokee Indians that were listed on the Dawes Rolls.

After much debate and controversy, in 2006, the law was ruled unconstitutional by the Cherokee Nation's Judicial Appeals Tribunal (now called the Cherokee Supreme Court).

After leaving office, Mankiller remained active in causes affecting women's and Native American rights. In 1987, *Ms.* magazine named her Woman of the Year. In 1993, she was inducted into the National Women's Hall of Fame and in 1998, was awarded the Presidential Medal of Freedom by President Bill Clinton.

Her writings include *Every Day Is a Good Day: Reflections by Contemporary Indigenous Women* (with Vine Deloria, Jr. and Gloria

Steinem), and her national bestselling autobiography, *Mankiller: A Chief and Her People* (with Michael Wallis).
http://en.wikipedia.org/wiki/Special:BookSources/1555915167

When she died in April 2010, President Barack Obama remarked that, as the Cherokee Nation's first female chief, Wilma Mankiller "... served as an inspiration to women in Indian country and across America. Her legacy will continue to encourage and motivate all who carry on her work."

38 NICOLE MATTHEWS, EXECUTIVE DIRECTOR, MIWSAC, SPEAKER, ADVOCATE

- Champion of Native female victims of sexual violence

A member of the White Earth Reservation, Nicole Matthews (Anishinabe) is executive director of the Minnesota Indian Women's Sexual Assault Coalition (MIWSAC), a statewide alliance for American Indian sexual assault victims advocates.

Its mission is to strengthen the voices of American Indian women to create awareness, influence social change, and reclaim the traditional values that honor the sovereignty of American Indian women and children. Through their vision, which is "to create safety and justice for Native women through the teachings of our grandmothers," MIWSAC works to eliminate sexual violence perpetrated against them.

She received her bachelor of science degree in applied psychology with minors in human relations and multicultural education from St. Cloud State University. Prior to her employment with MIWSAC, she was sexual assault services coordinator for the Mille Lacs County (Minnesota) Pearl Crisis Center.

Matthews has traveled to Tribal communities across the country to assist them in developing and strengthening their response to Native victims of sexual violence. She has worked with members of the coalition to produce public service announcements; has been invited to the White House to commemorate Domestic Violence Awareness Month; and was a panelist at the Department of Justice with the US attorney general during Sexual Assault Awareness Month.

As one of five researchers, Matthews and her team interviewed 105 Native American women used in prostitution and trafficking to prepare their report, *Garden of Truth: The Prostitution and Trafficking of Native Women in Minnesota.* Since the release of the report, she has spoken at many locations and venues, including New York City during the United Nations Commission on the Status of Women events.

Nicole Matthews credits her three children, Jazmin, Kiora, and Kionte with giving her the strength and motivation to continue her work to end violence against women and children.

EXTRA: NATIVE WOMEN AND VIOLENT CRIME

Native American women experience the highest levels of violent crimes against them than any other group in the United States.

The National Organization for Women (NOW) reports on its website that, according to American Indians and Crime (released by the Department of Justice), American Indian women experience violence at a rate three-and-a-half times more often than the national average.

They are also frequent victims of sexual and domestic violence, and as women of color, experience institutionalized racism at a higher rate than any other group. Alex Wilson, researcher for Indigenous Perspectives, a Native American group, found that Native American Indian women were also more likely to be treated by law enforcement as untruthful when they reported crimes.

Furthermore, in reservation communities, according to the American Indian Women's Chemical Health Project, they experience the highest levels of sexual and domestic abuse than any other group. And most remain silent due to fear of being alienated by their families, cultural hindrances, mistrust of Euro-American dominated agencies, and a history of lack of action by tribal and state agencies to prosecute crimes against them.

---

39 MARJORIE MURDOCK, BUSINESS MANAGER

- Operations Manager, Murdock Electricity and Maintenance Company
- Premier electrical company began in family's garage

Operations Manager for Murdock Electricity and Maintenance Company Marjorie Murdock holds a job that can cover planning, coordinating, and monitoring the work of various areas, departments, and operations. It can also involve supervising and reviewing financial data, ensuring and improving the efficiency and profitability of operations through providing effective methods and strategies—and more.

Based in Pine Ridge, South Dakota Murdock Electricity, a Native American family and veteran-owned business, began in Frank and Marjorie Murdock's garage in 1982. It is now the premier electrical services provider in southwest South Dakota, and operates with a staff of forty-five persons.

It was one of only six local Native contractors selected for the 93,642 square-foot, 28.5 million dollar Justice Center. Construction began in April 2012 to house the jail, police force, and judicial system for the Oglala Sioux.

One of the long-standing barriers to reservation-based Native American Indian businesses has been that much of reservation lands are held in trust by the Federal Government, which prohibits owners from using their property as collateral for loans.

With more than 30 years of business savvy, the Murdocks secured a Lakota Funds line of credit for an additional $200,000, which gave them the competitive edge over other Native American companies faced with land trust and levels of bonding issues.

Extra: Lakota Funds

As the first certified Native American community development financial institution on a reservation, since its inception in 1986, Lakota Funds has loaned more than six million dollars, created 1,235 jobs, and nearly 450 businesses on or near the Pine Ridge Indian Reservation.

It has provided training and services to over 1,600 artists, more than 1,200 aspiring entrepreneurs, and made available more goods and services than ever to community residents.

---

40 Ann Curry (b. 1956), National News Broadcaster

- Winner, Five Emmy Awards

Born in Guam (United States) to Bob Curry (Cherokee/multi-racial), a career Navy man, and Hiroe Nagase, a Japanese national, Ann lived in Japan for several years as a child and attended the Ernest J. King School on the Sasebo military base. Her mother was a Catholic convert and Ann was reared in the faith.

The family later moved to Ashland, Oregon, where Ann graduated from Ashland High School. She attended the University of Oregon and earned a bachelor of arts degree in journalism (1978).

Curry's broadcasting career began in the same year at NBC affiliate KTVL in Medford, Oregon. As an intern, she became the station's first female news reporter. She moved to NBC-affiliate KGW in Portland as reporter and anchor (1980). Four years later, Curry moved to Los Angeles, and as a reporter for KCBS-TV (1984-1990), received two Emmy Awards.

She joined NBC News as the News correspondent (1990) and moved quickly through the system to become anchor of *NBC News at Sunrise* (1991-1996). She was *Today* substitute news anchor for Matt Lauer (1994-1997), progressed to news anchor for *Today* (1997-2011), and, behind Frank Blair (1953-1975), became the show's second longest news anchor.

The *Today* segment, "Ann on the Run," followed her around as she read news on *Today*, taped *Dateline*, and filled in live for Brian Williams on *Nightly News*.

Curry has also filed stories from Sri Lanka, Baghdad, Rwanda, Democratic Republic of Congo, and other major areas of international news.

She has amassed five Emmy Awards, four Golden Mics, Associated Press certificates of excellence, three Gracie Allen awards, and the NAACP Excellence in Reporting Award. Curry has also received the Simon Wiesenthal Medal of Valor for coverage of the Darfur crisis and awards from Americares, Anti-Defamation League, Save the Children, Asian American Journalists Association, and other charities and organizations.

In 2010, after delivering the commencement address, Curry was awarded an honorary doctorate degree from Southern Oregon University. She has also been awarded honorary degrees from Providence College and Wheaton College.

After much controversy, in June 2012, Curry left *Today* as news anchor to become *NBC News* national and international correspondent/anchor, *Today* anchor-at-large, and heads a seven-person unit that produces content and reporting for *NBC Nightly News* with Brian Williams.

She anchors several *NBC News* primetime specials and is a regular substitute anchor for *Dateline NBC*, *Rock Center* with Brian Williams, *MSNBC*, and *Today*.

Ann Curry lives in New York City with her husband, Brian Ross, a software executive, and their two children, McKenzie and William.

41 PATSY PHILLIPS, MUSEUM DIRECTOR

- Founding member, Indigenous Arts Action Alliance

Patsy Phillips directs the only museum in the country dedicated solely to advancing the discourse, knowledge, and understanding of contemporary Native arts of North America.

Founded in 1972 and based in Santa Fe, New Mexico, the Museum of Contemporary Native Arts (MoCNA) houses the world's largest collection of contemporary Native American art. Its exhibits, programs, and collections encourage expression across fields and cultures and fosters dialogue across local, national, and global communities.

An enrolled member of the Cherokee Nation, Tahlequah, Oklahoma, Phillips manages a staff of twenty. Along with overseeing the Museum Standing Committee for formulation of policy and procedures, she supervises and evaluates programs that support its mission, goals, and priorities. Phillips also plans, monitors, and expends the museum's budget.

She earned her MA degree in writing from Johns Hopkins University, a graduate certificate in museum studies from Harvard University, and a BA degree in anthropology from Southern Methodist University.

From 2000 to 2008, she served at the Smithsonian's National Museum of the American Indian (NMAI). Among her several positions there, she was Development Officer and Director of Special Relationships with major donors. She also managed contemporary art initiatives.

The programs encompassed national and international projects that included key departments for the museum's three facilities: the National Mall in Washington DC, George Gustav Heye Center, New York City, and the Cultural Resources Center in Suitland, Maryland. In addition, Phillips managed the Indigenous Contemporary Arts program, which provided financial awards to Native arts and cultures, and initiated, developed and participated in the NMAI's strategic plan for contemporary art.

She is a founding member of the Indigenous Arts Action Alliance (IA3), an independent group of Native artists, educators, scholars and administrators. The group advocates for the advancement and understanding of contemporary Native American arts.

EXTRA: MUSEUM OF CONTEMPORARY NATIVE ARTS

In a Nutshell: The Museum of Contemporary Native Arts (MoCNA) is located in downtown Santa Fe. Formerly the Institute of American Indian Arts (IAIA), its collection evolved from a student honors program. Donations from private collectors and outside artists also enabled the formation of a museum in 1972. With no building of its own, art exhibits were held in borrowed space at the Santa Fe Indian School campus.

In January 1990, IAIA acquired the neglected Federal Building in the heart of downtown Santa Fe and in 2004, architects faced the challenge of refurbishing the 1922 Pueblo Revival style exterior and transforming its interior into a series of classrooms and galleries to house its collection of contemporary Native art.

In mid-2005, the museum reopened in its new setting that showcased Native art, cross-cultural dialogue, and educational programs.

MoCNA presently houses the premier collection in the world from Native American, First Nation and other Indigenous peoples. The nearly 7,500 artworks in the collection include sculpture, cultural arts, paintings, ceramics, works on paper, jewelry, contemporary apparel, photography, textiles, new media, and installations.

ALPHA PI OMEGA FOUNDERS:

42 CHRISTINA STRICKLAND (THEODOROU)
43 JAMIE GOINS
44 SHANNON BRAYBOY
45 AMY LOCKLEAR (HERTEL)

- Founded oldest and largest of historically Native American Greek letter organizations
- Sorority supports National Indian Education Association

Alpha Pi Omega, Inc. was founded on September 1, 1994, by four students at the University of North Carolina-Chapel

Hill: Christina Strickland (Theodorou), Jamie Goins, Shannon Brayboy, and Amy Locklear (Hertel).

In the spring of 1995, it pledged its first class of sisters, known as the Fifteen Warrior Women, and in the fall, received its incorporation status.

Known to the membership as the Four Winds, each co-founder experienced times when she felt alienated from the rest of the students attending the university. During Brayboy's sophomore year, she attended other Native organizations on campus, but none fulfilled the specific needs of Native American Indian women. She did, however, meet three others who shared similar needs to connect.

Because they had witnessed other Native Indian students drop out because of homesickness and feelings of alienation, Brayboy, Goins, Strickland, and Locklear, all members of the Lumbee Tribe, decided that only the closeness and sisterhood of a sorority could fulfill the void that other groups could not.

They established Alpha Pi Omega's mission principles to reflect their specific needs: respecting Native traditions, lending support to one another, self-renewal through continuous education, giving honor to the Creator, and focusing on critical issues that face both Native communities and society as a whole. The National Indian Education Association is the sorority's national philanthropy.

With more than seventy tribes now represented among its nearly five hundred members nationwide, Alpha Pi Omega's membership is open to women at the undergraduate and postgraduate level.

According to Grand Director, Lenzy Krehbiel-Burton, as of June 2012, active undergraduate chapters are chartered at UNC-Chapel Hill; UNC-Pembroke; Oklahoma State University; University of New Mexico; Dartmouth College; North Carolina State University; Northeastern (Oklahoma) State University; and Arizona State University. Graduate chapters are chartered in North Carolina and Oklahoma.

In July 2012, the sorority established a provisional undergraduate chapter at Oregon State University and provisional graduate chapters in the District of Columbia and Bernalillo County, New Mexico.

Additional expansion sites include Dane County, Wisconsin (graduate); University of Wisconsin-Madison; Northern Colorado University; Harvard University; Haskell Indian Nations University; Western Carolina University; the University of Kansas; Western Carolina University; and the University of North Dakota.

EXTRA: ALPHA PI OMEGA

The sorority is governed nationally by a twelve-member board known as the Grand Keepers of the Circle. Its colors are Fire Red, New Grass Green, and Maize Yellow. The queen bee, amethyst gem, cedar tree, and dogwood flower are its official symbols.

The Tribes represented on the board as of June 2012, include the Cherokee Nation, Choctaw Nation, Lumbee Tribe, Menominee, and Muscogee (Creek).

All four founders remain active within the sorority.

---

46 TAWNEY BRUNSCH, EXECUTIVE DIRECTOR, LAKOTA FUNDS

- Executive Director of Lakota Funds
- Chairperson, Federal Credit Union Steering Committee

Oglala Sioux tribal member Tawney Brunsch grew up on a ranch south of the interior on the Pine Ridge Indian Reservation. She attended grade school through middle school at Interior Elementary and graduated from Wall High School. She attended South Dakota State University where she earned her bachelor of science degree in commercial economics, was active in the Econ Club, and graduated with Omicron Delta Epsilon honors—an international economics honor society.

She is the executive director of Lakota Funds, the first certified Reservation-based Native community development financial institution, and has held several finance-related positions: portfolio manager at Lakota Funds; has eight years experience at Black Hills

Federal Credit Union, Wall (South Dakota) branch manager; successfully juggled positions of loan officer, teller, branch security manager, collection officer and staff motivator. All at the same time. In 2007, Brunsch was named Wall Neighborhood Housing Services Volunteer of the Year, and served on the Economic Development Committee in Wall.

Brunsch is a certified volunteer income tax assistance preparer, and also serves on the Board of Directors for Mazaska Owecaso Otipi Financial.

In addition, Tawney Brunsch is Federal Credit Union Steering Committee Chairperson. The first of its kind on the Pine Ridge Reservation, it began accepting deposits in November 2012.

47 Rhonda LeValdo, Semi-Finalist

- International YouTube/Pulitzer Center Project Report Video Competition
- News story aired on C-SPAN

Acoma Pueblo tribal member, Rhonda LeValdo, is currently a faculty member in the Media Communications Department at Haskell Indian Nations University in Lawrence, Kansas, and advisor for the student newspaper, *Indian Leader*. She also hosts *Native Spirit Radio* on KKFI 901FM in Kansas City.

Along with her research partner, Teresa Lamsam, LeValdo recently launched a website, Wellboundstorytellers.com, to encourage other Native Americans to begin living healthy lifestyles. When time permits, she is an occasional contributor to *News from Indian Country* newspaper, Lastrealindians.com, and ndnsports.com.

A member of the Native American Journalists Association, in 2007, LeValdo was elected to its board of directors. She served as vice president (2008-2009). In 2010, she was elected president and served until her term expired in 2013.

Involved in all facets of media, she completed the documentary, *The Kickapoo Cultural Experience: The Kickapoo of Kansas*

(2007). The film won the Kanza Film Festival Documentary Film category, and was shown on the PBS-Topeka affiliate in the summer of that year. It was also selected for the thirtieth annual American Indian Film Festival in San Francisco.

LeValdo was named one of twenty-three KU Women of Distinction for a number of projects at Haskell and NAJA (2009-2010); she was also awarded a National Minority Consortia $10,000 fellowship (where she produced three video segments for *PBS Online Newshour*).

In a 2008 competition, LeValdo was selected as one of ten semi-finalists for an international YouTube/Pulitzer Center Project Report video competition.

The contest garnered LeValdo much attention throughout the United States, including a guest spot on the C-SPAN show, *Close Up at the Newseum*, where her news story was aired regarding the Federal Government's obligations to American Indian students, particularly at Haskell Indian Nations University.

Rhonda LeValdo is married to Denny Gayton and they have two children: Hepanna and Winona. The family resides in Lawrence, Kansas.

---

48 DIANE HUMETEWA, ATTORNEY

- First Native American female US Attorney

In 2007 Diane Humetewa became the first ever Native American woman in United States history to be presidentially appointed as United States attorney in any state. Under the George W. Bush administration, she served in the position from 2007 to 2009.

A member of the Hopi tribe, Diane Humetewa (hoo-MEE-tee-wah) was born and reared in Arizona and started school on the Hualapai Reservation. Her father worked for the Bureau of Indian Affairs and often took Diane with him as he traveled throughout Indian country. The trips exposed young Diane to Arizona's tribes at an early age.

Although she attended public high school at a time when many

Indian children were sent to boarding schools far from their reservations, her ties to her family and culture kept her close to the Hopi Reservation.

She is a two-time graduate of Arizona State University (ASU) where she earned her BA degree (1987) and her JD degree (1993) from the Sandra Day O'Connor College of Law. She has served on its College of Law Indian Legal Advisory Committee since 1997. She is a member of the Arizona State Bar Association and was Appellate Court Judge for the Hopi Indian Tribe.

In her early career, Humetewa helped to establish one of the first federal victim services programs in the nation. She represented tribal governments as an attorney specializing in federal Indian, and natural resources law. She was also counsel to the US Senate Indian Affairs Subcommittee, then chaired by Senator John McCain.

As Assistant US Attorney, Humetewa prosecuted a wide variety of federal crimes, violent crimes in Indian country, and Native American and archeological resource crimes. She was counsel to the deputy attorney general for the US Justice Department and deputy counsel for the US Senate on Indian Affairs.

In 2011, Humetewa joined the ASU administrative and legal team, and is a professor of practice with the ASU Sandra Day O'Connor College of Law. Humetewa is Special Advisor on American Indian Affairs to ASU President Michael Crow, and Special Counsel for the Office of General Counsel. In addition, she works to build ASU's relationships with Indian tribal governments.

Her duties further include chairperson of the ASU Tribal Liaison Advisory Committee, service on the Provost's Native American Advisory Council, and promotion of higher education opportunities among Arizona's tribes, while continuing the recruitment and retention of new ASU students from Native American communities.

Among her awards, distinctions and achievements, in 2009, Humetewa received the President's Award, the highest honorary distinction of Women in Federal Law Enforcement, in recognition of her outstanding career achievement as a prosecutor, crime victims' advocate, and her dedication to the training of law enforcement agents to improve their response to crimes committed on tribal lands.

Diane Humetewa is also listed in *48 Intriguing Women of Arizona*.

49 MARY HUDETZ, PRESIDENT, NATIVE AMERICAN JOURNALISTS ASSOCIATION

- Mentored Native American Journalists Association student projects

Mary Hudetz (Crow) grew up on the Crow Agency in Montana and currently lives in Phoenix, Arizona.

Hudetz has studied dance extensively at the Ailey School and earned a BFA at the Ailey/Fordham BFA Program. She also studied at the North Carolina School of the Arts and has performed as a company dancer in the North Carolina Dance Theatre 2, and in works by prestigious choreographers including Alvin Ailey, Judith Jamison, Igal Perry, and Paul Taylor.

When her interest shifted to writing, Hudetz entered the Freedom Forum's American Indian Journalism Institute (AIJI), and the School of Journalism at the University of Montana for graduate studies (2006).

In 2007, she was chosen a Chips Quinn Scholar, a program that, according to its website, provides for "diversity in journalism and offers students hands-on training and mentoring by caring news veterans."

Hudetz, herself, has mentored Native American Journalists Association (NAJA) student projects in Minneapolis, has served at the Crazy Horse Journalism Workshop, and teaches at the AIJI.

Among her many other skills, she is endorsed for copy editing, journalism, blogging, feature writing, and investigative reporting.

She joined the West Desk in June 2009, was an advisor on the Associated Press (AP) Native Peoples Beat Team, and is currently

AP West Regional Desk editor (Phoenix). Hudetz also files national breaking news on a number of other topics, has served as interim member of the NAJA board of directors, and as its vice president.

In July 2013, Mary Hudetz was elected to a three-year term as president of the Native American Journalists Association.

NAJA EXTRA

In 1983 a group of thirty Native American journalists convened at Pennsylvania State University to assess the status of Native Media, and discuss ways to nurture and develop Native communications. They reconvened in early 1984 at the Choctaw Nation of Oklahoma, created a constitution and by-laws, and established the Native American Press Association (NAPA).

In 1990 the organization was renamed the Native American Journalists Association (NAJA), in order to include radio and television professionals within its membership.

NAJA is based in Norman, Oklahoma. A 501(c)(3) tax-exempt status organization, it strives to improve communications among Native peoples and between Native Americans and the general public.

V.

ARTISTS, CRAFTSPERSONS, AND DESIGNERS

BEADWORK, BASKETRY, POTTERY, AND MANY OTHER works help to preserve heritage and culture, while sharing with the world the beauty of Native American Indian craftsmanship.

And, then, there are those whose visions soar far beyond the boundaries of tradition.

NINE LAKOTA STAR QUILT ARTISTS

- Their handmade Star Quilts preserve a Lakota Tradition

Crafts have long been an intricate and honored part of Native American cultures. With the Lakota, star quilts are valued gifts and popular collector's items. They are often seen at powwows and sometimes in gift shops.

To receive a star quilt as a present has a deep and personal meaning and is a great honor. These nine Lakota star quilt artists fashion their beautiful crafts as part of their home businesses and as gifts on special occasions. Except for Cheryl Arguello and Norma Blacksmith, the following information, some edited for reasons of space, is provided through the quilters' websites.

50 Vera Good Lance (b. 1933)

Lifetime Oglala resident, Vera Good Lance began making baby blankets in a nine-design block style at age seventeen. They were given as gifts for Naming ceremonies when a child or grandchild is given a Lakota name, which is passed down from their grandparents. Many of her relatives make star and block quilts.

Vera has three brothers, one sister, eight children, forty-seven grandchildren and twenty-nine great-grandchildren: P.O. Box 201, Oglala, South Dakota 57764 (605) 867-1063.

51 L. Pansy Two Bulls Weasel Bear (b. 1961)

An Oglala Lakota tribal member from the Pine Ridge Indian Reservation in South Dakota, hers is the Tatanka Nunpa Tiospaye.

L. Pansy became tired of buying star quilts for cultural honoring, graduations, Hunka ceremonies, and other occasions, so she began to make her own. Her first was for their third daughter, Mary, at her high school graduation.

She also makes ribbon and ceremonial dresses, shirts for men, fancy shawl outfits, and beaded butterflies. She looks forward to growth of her small family business that helps to provide for the family's necessities. Contact L. Pansy: P.O. Box 894, Pine Ridge, South Dakota 57770 (605) 867-1853; Cell: (605) 407-0996

52 Leola One Feather (1954)

Leola was born on the Pine Ridge Indian Reservation. She learned sewing from her mother, Mary One Feather. She played with her mother's treadle sewing machine at age seven (and broke lots of needles!). Her mother's patience kept her interested in sewing and she made her first star quilt, a candy cane design, at age fifteen, which she kept for her own bed.

The star quilts that Leola now makes on request have special meaning for her and are a beautiful reflection of Lakota culture. She also likes to make star quilt clothing and design dance outfits. Leola further enjoys making small beadwork accessories such as lighter wraps, key chain holders and hair ties.

Her master sewing techniques include southern-style ribbon work and quill work. She also crafts beautiful Indian dolls accented with beadwork and is experienced in hide-tanning and painting. She has eight children and sixteen grandchildren.

Contact: P.O. Box 12, Wounded Knee, South Dakota 57794 (605) 867-2654.

53 GERMAINE MOVES CAMP (1958)

Born in Pine Ridge, South Dakota, to Ellen Winter Moves Camp, Germaine is a descendent of the great Lakota Chief Red Cloud and a long lineage of medicine men on her father's side. She has five children: three boys, two girls, and five grandchildren.

Germaine learned star quilting from her mother at age eighteen. At age twenty, she made her first full quilt. For a memorial, she helped her mother to make twenty-five quilts in fourteen days. Germaine explains that star quilts are made for people during their hard times or to honor them.

Contact: (605) 462-5002; (605) 685-3829.

54 WILMA THIN ELK (B.1938)

A full-blood Lakota, Wilma was born in the Pine Ridge Hospital, Rocky Ford Wakan Community. Both of her parents were also born on the reservation.

She began sewing at fourteen after a Womanhood Ceremony (considered very sacred), and later began making star blankets and quilts for her children. The star, she explains, is symbolic of Christ's birth, and guided the three wise men to Bethlehem. The explanation, she states, was passed down by her grandmother.

Wilma's quilts also earn extra money for her and her family. She also makes specialty quilts such as the Buffalo, Medicine Wheel, and Bronco Rider.

She makes quilts for funeral memorials, graduations, and births. Wilma also makes satin quilts and agreed to teach the art to others in her community. She quilts by hand, and machine marks the top.

Wilma has four children, is rearing three of her eight grandchildren and one great-grandson in her Manderson, South Dakota home.

Contact Wilma: General Delivery, Pine Ridge, South Dakota 57770 (605) 867-2788; Cell: (650) 454-1400.

55 Ernestine Joyce Bell (b. 1929)

Ernestine is an Oglala Lakota tribal member from Pine Ridge, South Dakota. She was born in Sturgis and grew up in Slim Buttes (both in South Dakota). Her parents, Bessie Brings and Ed Red Feather, are both full-blood Lakota.

Ernestine learned to make star quilts from her mother and grandmother when she was ten years old. She fashions them for ceremonies, newborns, graduations, giveaways, memorials, and other occasions.

Contact: Box 125, Pine Ridge, South Dakota 57770 (605) 867-2185.

56 REGINA BRAVE
(1941)

She was born in Oglala to Milton and Sarah (Belt) Brave. She attended boarding school at Holy Rosary Mission (now known as Red Cloud), where she learned to cut from patterns when she was twelve years old. At fourteen, she could make school uniforms in various sizes.

A self-taught star quilt maker since 1970, Regina knows crochet, embroidery, and cross-stitch. Also since the 1970s, she has made ribbon shirts, vests, dance outfits, and embroidered her own Native designs in her quilts.

Regina moved to Denver in 1976 and began making and marketing the Broken Star with or without matching pillow shams, and also wall hangings, shower curtains, and drapes. She returned to the reservation in 1999.

Her inspiration is her mother, whose parents were Frank and Lizzy Walks Out Belt. When Lizzy was in her 70s, Regina remembers how she hitchhiked to work for the Foster Grandparents Program in Pine Ridge. At age 80, she auditioned for and was cast in the role of Maizie Blue Legs in the movie, *Thunderheart*.

Regina remembers that her grandmother always made star quilts on a Singer treadle sewing machine, and beginning in 1960, her crafts were Lizzy's only source of income. Her last star quilt was made for actor Val Kilmer in 1992.

In her year of mourning, Regina began to design and copyright her numerous original contemporary and traditional designs in the diamonds of the star quilts.

As a US Navy veteran (who was also at Wounded Knee in 1973), Regina added the Marine Corps emblem in the diamond, entered the quilt in the 2006 Veterans Creative Arts local art show in Hot Springs, South Dakota, and was awarded First Place.

Regina's dream is to have a star quilt show for all the Oglala Lakota star quilt artists and turn it into an annual event.

Regina has four children, nine grandchildren and two great-grandchildren. Contact: P.O. Box 512, Oglala, South Dakota 57764 (605) 454-5674.

57 CHERYL ARGUELLO (B. 1959)

Cheryl is a soon-to-be ordained minister who serves Native American people in Pierre, South Dakota, Cheyenne Reservation. She also does outreach on the Rosebud Reservation. Cheryl enjoys quilting in her spare time and learned the craft from her mother.

She does not yet have a website, but you may contact her at: 715 S. Buchanan Ave., Pierre, SD 57501 (605) 381-5638.

58 NORMA BLACKSMITH

Norma's quilting business is located adjacent to Pine Ridge in Whiteclay, Nebraska. Contact: (605) 441-2090.

For images of Lakota star quilts, visit: lakotaquilts.com

59 JUDY BAKER (B. 1943), SEMINOLE PALMETTO DOLL ARTIST

- Descended from generations of doll crafters

Judy Baker learned the craft of making Seminole palmetto dolls from her grandmother and mother, and began making them herself at around ten years of age.

She explains that palmetto dolls are made from fiber that is found in the middle of palmetto bark. Brown in color, it stretches after being cut, and when dried, can then be fashioned into dolls.

Palmetto is harvested from thickets where it grows by using tools such as axes, knives, saws, and sometimes files. One palmetto plant yields between four and five dolls. According to Baker, the first Seminole dolls, made around 1900, were toys for children, and were not clothed. Although Baker's directions for doll-making sound simple enough, the end product is quite intricate in its beauty.

"The head is made first and stuffed with palmetto fibers. The body was traditionally stuffed with palmetto fiber also, although sometimes cotton is used," she states. "A circle of cardboard is cut for the bottom to keep the doll steady when standing it.

"The face is fashioned by embroidering or sewing on the eyes and mouth. The hair is sometimes made from cardboard and black fabric in the style once worn by traditional women. The hair may also be fashioned from yarn in ponytails and braided styles.

"Sometimes the doll's hair is crafted in the 'board' or 'bonnet' hairstyle. Although virtually unseen now, Seminole women once fanned their hair over a tilted cardboard disk-shaped frame that was stabilized by the hair once in place.

"When the tourist boom began in Miami, Florida, at around the 1920s, visitors loved to see the Seminole villages. Although they enjoyed exhibitions and entertainment such as alligator wrestling and could purchase souvenir beads and other crafts, the palmetto dolls were a favorite."

Doll-making quickly became a cottage industry that earned income for the Seminoles. Clothing was added in the colorful, elaborate patchwork and other traditional designs along with beads and earrings.

The dolls are available on the six Seminole reservations throughout Florida, at annual powwows and crafts shows, and the Tribe's gift shop at Ah Tah Thi Ki Museum, Big Cypress Reservation. But, Judy Baker and other doll artists sometimes make the highly prized dolls by special request.

For colorful images, visit: Seminole Indian Palmetto Dolls.

EXTRA: SEMINOLE PATCHWORK

The artistry of Seminole Patchwork began during difficult times for the Seminole when women used scraps and leftover fabric to fashion into hand-made clothing. As early as 1880, Seminole seamstresses acquired hand-operated sewing machines. A dozen years later, an explorer spotted the machines in every Seminole camp he visited in southeast Florida.

The colorful patchwork garments were first made from strips of cloth in horizontal patterns of contrasting colors for both men and women shortly before 1920. They eventually evolved into a series of "stock" or "traditional" patterns: the disagree symbol; bones; diamondback rattlesnake; tree; crawfish; rain; lightning/ thunder; broken arrow; man on horse; bird; and four directions medicine colors.

Designs may also symbolize Seminole clans, which are matrilineal: Panther, Bird, Wind, Otter, Bear, Snake, Deer, and Toad/Bigtown.

As time passed, creative symbols unique to the designer also became a trend. Seminole patchwork designs are seen on skirts, jackets, vests, and other types of clothing. It is also used to fashion potholders, bonnets, purses, totes, towels, quilts, and many other items.

To be gifted with a Seminole handcraft is a great honor.

---

60 Frida Kahlo
(1907-1954), Painter

- One of Mexico's greatest Surrealist painters

Born Magdalena Carmen Frida Kahlo y Calderon in Coyoacan, Mexico, Frida was the third of four daughters born to Guillermo Kahlo (Carl Wilhelm Kahlo of Pforzheim, Germany) and Matilde Calderon y Gonzalez, a devout Roman Catholic of Native American/Spanish ancestry.

Frida Kahlo was widely known for her long colorful skirts, that, more than a creative statement, concealed a right leg thinner than the left due to polio contracted when she was six years old. It was one of several adversities Kahlo would suffer in her lifetime.

As an eighteen-year-old premed student, the collision of a bus on which she was riding resulted in a fractured spinal column, ribs, pelvis, and several bones in her right leg. She also sustained other injuries that resulted in her inability to bring three pregnancies to term.

During a convalescence lasting longer than a year, Frida turned to art. Her mother had a special easel constructed to facilitate her painting in bed and her father supplied oil paints and brushes. It set the course for the self-taught artist to evolve into one of Mexico's greatest surrealist painters.

When she met renowned Mexican muralist, Diego Rivera, in 1927, he encouraged her to develop her talent, and strongly influenced her decision to pursue art as a career.

Although 20 years his junior, they married in 1929 when Frida was only 22. The marriage was a tempestuous one. They divorced and remarried, but the union remained troubled.

Many of her works reflected the angst of her marriage, her sufferings. Of her 143 paintings, 55 of them are self-portraits that suggest pain. In her primitive style, Kahlo utilized the bright colors and dramatic symbolism that reflected Mexican culture. Monkeys, symbols of lust in Mexican mythology, were reinterpreted by Kahlo as tender and protective.

At the invitation of Andre Breton (French writer and poet, author of the first *Surrealist Manifesto*), Kahlo exhibited her painting, *The Frame*, at the Louvre in Paris in 1939. It was the first work of a 20th century Mexican artist to be acquired by the prestigious gallery.

Known largely as the wife of Diego Rivera during her lifetime, it was not until May 1982 during the rise of the *neomexicanismo* style, that the first Frida Kahlo retrospective was held—not in Mexico, but in London's Whitechapel Gallery. Others exhibits followed in Sweden, Germany, Manhattan—and Mexico City.

Frida, Naturaleza Viva, the 1983 movie about her life, was hugely successful. A biography by Hayden Herrera, *Frida: The Biography of Frida Kahlo*, along with other biographies, became worldwide bestsellers that further contributed to her posthumous popularity.

Following her death, her family home, *Casa Azul* (Blue House), where she grew up and returned in her final years, was donated by Diego Rivera (who died three years after Frida) as a museum for the artifacts of her life and is a popular tourist attraction.

Frida Kahlo's works are now exhibited in museums worldwide.

Her many works include *My Birth* (1932); *Self-Portrait with Monkey* (1938); *The Two Fridas* (1939); *Self-Portrait With Thorn Necklace and Hummingbird* (1940); *Without Hope* (1945); and *Diego and I* (1949).

---

61 PATRICIA MICHAELS (B. 1967)
FASHION DESIGNER

- First Native American designer to show collection at New York Fashion Week

When one thinks of Native American fashion design, traditional aesthetics usually come to mind in the forms of intricate beading, silver and turquoise, fringe and feathers—styles that have deviated little over time. But Patricia Michaels (Taos Pueblo/Polish descent), based in Taos, New Mexico, has taken her edgy and sophisticated fashions into the mainstream.

She grew up between Santa Fe, where her parents operated their art gallery and Taos Pueblo. She was educated at the Institute of American Indian Arts and the Chicago Art Institute, and while she respects and is inspired by iconic mainstays, she also draws insight from both her heritage and the contemporary. Her sometimes ethereal designs "nurture, compliment and celebrate the feminine form at any age," she states on her website.

Her artistry is achieved through the mastery of a number of methods, among them, blending her own dyes and manipulating textiles. She may burn holes in her fabrics to distress them, silk screen or paint on them by hand. Michaels may also integrate fabrics as dissimilar as felted wool and silk organza.

Michaels has shared in cultural exchanges from as near as Santa Fe's Indian Market, to as far away as New Zealand, in order to expand her experiences with different shapes, textures, and other elements of her designs.

In 2011, Patricia Michaels became the first Native American Indian designer to show her collection at New York Fashion Week.

Contact: h2owaterlily@gmail.com

62 WILDFIRE (MARY EDMONIA LEWIS, CA. 1843-1907), SCULPTOR

- First female sculptor of Native American descent

More broadly known as Mary Edmonia Lewis, Wildfire was born in Greenbush, New York, was one of two children of an Ojibway (Chippewa) mother, and a father of West Indian descent. She spent her early childhood with her mother's people, the Mississauga Band of Ojibway Indians.

After she and her brother, Sunrise (Samuel W. Lewis), were orphaned when she was around ten years old, two aunts reared them in northern New York State.

Sunrise, who was twelve years Wildfire's senior, joined the Gold Rush and with the riches he obtained, financed Wildfire's education to a preparatory school. Later, in 1859, she attended Oberlin College (Ohio) where she studied literature. It was there that Wildfire changed her name to "Mary Edmonia," although she seldom used "Mary."

While attending Oberlin, she was accused by two Euro-American women students of attempting to poison them. Even though she was acquitted, she was verbally attacked, beaten by vigilantes, and Oberlin refused to allow her to re-enroll the following year to complete studies for her degree.

She moved to New York and studied with sculptor, Edward Brackett. Copies of her bust of Robert Gould Shaw, commander of the 54th Massachusetts Infantry, Union Army, was such a financial success, the proceeds enabled her to sail to Rome where she mastered working in stone in the neoclassical style.

It was also in Rome that she converted to Roman Catholicism (1868) and where she rendered *Forever Free* (1867), her best known work. Her last known major work was *Death of Cleopatra* (carved in 1876), and exhibited at the Centennial Exposition (1876) in Philadelphia, the first official World's Fair in the United States (http://en.wikipedia.org/wiki/Edmonia_Lewis).

Lewis' works sometimes depicted Native American Indians,

and although a friend to abolitionists, her refusal to abandon her Indian heritage in her works may have cost her patrons and possibly contributed to the decline in popularity of her sculptures.

Her preferred subjects also included biblical themes, freedom, famous Americans, and abolitionists. The costuming of her figures was considered ethnically accurate, but her works were criticized for the European features of her female figures.

Lewis disappeared from the American public sometime in the late 1880s and there have been several dates of her death with no documented evidence to support them.

Recently, however, cultural historian, Marilyn Richardson, located the documented date and place of her death. Mary Edmonia Lewis had been living in the Hammersmith area of London, died in the Hammersmith Borough Infirmary on September 17, 1907 and left a small estate.

The biblical Egyptian handmaid, *Hagar in the Wilderness* (1868) and *The Old Arrow Maker and His Daughter* (1872), which depicts two Native American figures are also among her best-known sculptures.

Her pieces are part of the Howard University Gallery of Art and the Smithsonian American Art Museum. Recent decades have experienced a renewed interest in her life and works.

63 Charlene Holy Bear, Doll Artist

- Award-winning master of eight different quillwork techniques

Charlene Holy Bear (Standing Rock Lakota Sioux) grew up largely in northern New Mexico. Instructed by her older sister, Rhonda, she created her first doll when she was only five years of age. In 1987 when she was seven, Charlene was encouraged to enter a doll in the youth juried competition. She was awarded second place. It would be the first of many prizes that she would amass, and the beginning of many exhibits of her work in prestigious galleries across the nation.

While attending high school at the Santa Fe Indian School, she continued to create dolls and entered several youth shows in the Mosi Lakai-Bi'kisi Gallery.

Along with her sister, she has also exhibited at the Morning Star Gallery in Santa Fe. As an adult, Holy Bear has participated in the Santa Fe Indian Market for a number of years and collected many awards and recognitions.

She studied fine arts and art history at the University of New Mexico (1997-2002) and has used that knowledge and experience to create historically-based dolls that demonstrate various aspects of Native American life. She was also 2008 recipient of a Southwestern Association for Indian Arts (SWAIA) Fellowship.

While she was hired to work with a private collection, in addition to learning how to restore, she also learned quillwork—ornamental creations in porcupine or bird quills. To date she has mastered eight different quillwork techniques. Her workmanship reflects her mastery of the intricate incorporation of quillwork and Lakota beadwork designs.

She also works in parfleche—dried animal skins—to render works that reflect both traditional and modern styles. A wonderful example of her contemporary creativity is the bold, unique, and nontraditional step Holy Bear takes in incorporating a beaded Oriental-style fan in one of her dancer's hands. The doll's body is fashioned from brain-tanned buckskin over wire, while the face is sculpted from cellulose clay.

"It took an entire year to create, and an additional two years to design the clothing and beadwork," Holy Bear states.

Her dolls are in a number of collections: the National Museum of the American Indian, Washington DC; the Foundation for the Preservation of American Indian Arts and Cultures; Chicago's Mitchell Museum, St. Augustine's Indian Center, and Father Peter Powell (Chicago).

Holy Bear has won many competitions. The Eiteljorg Museum (Indianapolis, Indiana) awarded her Best of Show, Best of Division, and First Place in the 19th Annual Eiteljorg Museum Indian Market and Festival. She also received the

Purchase Award for a beaded purse (June 2011). The following June she won Best of Division and first place in the 20th Annual Eiteljorg Museum Indian Market and Festival, and the Harrison Eiteljorg Purchase Award. In the same festival, one of her dolls was included in the Museum's permanent collection.

Her interview, *The Road to Indian Market 2010: Charlene Holy Bear 'Best in Class' Lakota Sioux Doll Maker'* can be viewed on YouTube.

Charlene Holy Bear with one of her expertly crafted dolls was the cover feature story in the 2012 May/June edition of *Native Peoples* magazine.

Email address: contact_me@charleneHoly Bear.com

---

64 Women Potters of San Marcos Tlapazola, Oaxaca

- They create pre-Hispanic-style pottery the old way

According to Alvin Starkman who has lived in Oaxaca since 2004, writes about its diverse cultural traditions, and conducts personal tours of the area, Sundays are busy days for the women of this small village. They may begin their day as early as 3 a.m. to prepare delicious beverages such as *tejate*, a corn and cacao-based drink to sell at the nearby Tlacolula marketplace.

To produce and market pre-Hispanic styled pottery including cups, plates, bowls, and other containers, as well as masks and figurines, together with in-laws, families sometimes form home-based enterprises. The young learn the ancient art from observing skilled elders and through serving as their apprentices.

The pottery and all that goes with its production is the core of their economic survival. On any day except Sunday, if the women do not purchase twigs and branches to kindle their oven fires to bake their pottery, they may be found searching the hillsides of their village for rotted logs, dried leaves, tumbleweed, and such. They bundle and tie them to the sides of their mules and bring them home.

They must also gather sand to mix with water. When it is pliable enough, they knead and form it into clay to fashion wares to sell at Tlacolula where tourists and native Oaxacans gather.

But before Sunday arrives, they busily apply their skills and resourcefulness: a corn cob to even surfaces and gourds to aid in the production of a desired shape. Strips of leather may be used to create a smooth finish and river stones smoothed by time may burnish the exterior of wares coated by a redder clay to produce a terra cotta tone.

While some Atzompa ceramic artisans use above-ground cement and brick ovens, others fashion their own below-ground brick-lined pits.

The women of San Marcos, however, may build their makeshift ovens from items as unlikely as a rusted wheelbarrow, a bicycle tire rim, broken pottery shards, a discarded bedspring—whatever will serve their purpose to bake their pottery.

After creating a circular base, they may place bedspring atop staggered layers of brick to allow for the circulation of air. Sheets of rusted and otherwise unusable metal are sometimes placed on the top and along the sides of the oven to control air entering the inside of the enclosed space—while always taking care to control the fire. A successful firing day means no rain or unduly high winds.

After the baking is completed and the wares have cooled, the women will disassemble the oven, remove, dust, and wrap them. Once placed in a box, they wait for their Sunday trip to the Tlacolula marketplace. Time to adorn themselves in headdresses and brightly colored embroidered taffeta frocks—traditional styles that set the women of Oaxaca apart from other villagers.

Once at the market, tourists and other Oaxacans, lured by aromas from the bakeries, enjoy chocolate-filled buns and other delicious pastries. Nearby, there's the church.

Compared to other days, market day is a time of rest, before the whole process begins anew, as the women fashioners of pre-Hispanic-style pottery continue the legacy of keeping the craft alive.

For complimentary pre-Hispanic recipes and more information, email Casa Machaya Oaxaca Bed & Breakfast at oaxacadream@hotmail.com or visit: http://www.casamachaya.com.

65 DAT SO LA LEE (B. CA. 1829, D. 1925) BASKET WEAVER

- Hers are among the world's most sought-after Native American baskets.

Born in Washoe Territory (California-Nevada border) Dat So La Lee, a Washoe Indian, was also known as Dabuda (Young Willow), her given name. Her English name was Louisa Keyser. Her father was Da Da Uongala, her mother's name is unrecorded. She lived in and around Carson City, Carson Valley, and Lake Tahoe. She became known as Dat So La Lee sometime around 1899.

Records show that her first husband was called Lame Tom and Assu, and that he probably died from consumption (tuberculosis). None of her children survived childhood. She laundered clothes and cooked for miners and their wives during her earlier years, and later for Abe Cohn (1859–1934) and his wife, Amy (1861–1919), who owned the Emporium Company Clothing Store in Carson City, Nevada.

When she married again, this time to Charlie Keyser (part Washoe Indian, and 24 years younger), she took yet another name, Louisa Keyser. In 1895, when Abe Cohn purchased four willow-covered bottles from her that she had woven in a fine art curio style, he noticed her great skill and became her sponsor, press agent, and business manager.

By 1899, Amy Cohn recorded each of Dat So La Lee's baskets in a ledger along with their dates, dimensions and designs. The ledger is preserved in the Nevada State Museum in Carson City where more than a dozen of her major works are housed.

Dat so La Lee also created a collection of miniature baskets and plainer twined baskets for souvenirs. Until Charlie's death (1928), the couple lived comfortably with the Cohns with all their expenses paid. In return for room and board, Dat So La Lee wove them her baskets.

She is probably best remembered for her degikup (day-gee-coop) baskets, a type that begins with a small circular base and extends up and out to a maximum circumference and then becomes smaller until the opening at top is the same dimension as the base. They were finely decorated with red and black redbud and bracken fern designs in scattered arrangements. She wove baskets for Cohn's Emporium until her death in 1925.

It is accepted that some of her artistry was possibly inspired by Pomo and Miwok Indians, but most were her own. She used symbols to tell the legends of her Tribe, and Dat So La Lee's works are among the world's most sought-after Native American baskets.

In 1922, a short documentary film was made about her work and Edward Sheriff Curtis (1868-1952), renowned photographer of the American West and Native American Indian peoples, photographed her at the Emporium.

Abe Cohn recognized the worth of her major pieces and demanded high prices. Even so, most of her works remained unsold at Abe Cohn's death in 1934. They were sold cheaply by his widow and second wife. Their value recovered in 1971.

---

66 ANGEL DECORA (1871–1919), ILLUSTRATOR, EDUCATOR,

- Illustrated for *Harper's Magazine*
  http://en.wikipedia.org/wiki/Harper%27s_Magazine

Hinook-Mahiwi-Kilinaka (Angel DeCora, Winnebago Tribe) was born in a wigwam on the Winnebago Reservation in what is now Thurston, Nebraska. Her Native name, Woman Coming on the Clouds in Glory, is a close translation of the English word, Angel.

Her father, David "Tall" DeCora (Winnebago/French), was son of Little DeCora, Chief of the Winnebago. Her mother, convent-educated, was of the prominent Winnebago LaMere family.

DeCora attended a Reservation school until age twelve, when, along with several other Winnebago boys and girls, she was sent east to Hampton Institute (Virginia).

Initially founded for African Americans, the racial demographics shifted in 1878 when seventeen former Plains warriors, captured years earlier and held as prisoners-of-war at Florida's Fort Marion, were admitted. Colonel Richard Henry Pratt, founder of the Carlisle Indian School, hoped that attending Hampton would make them "useful, law-abiding citizens."

During her five years at the institute, DeCora showed interest and skill in art and music. She returned to the reservation for a time, found it difficult to navigate the two worlds, and returned to Hampton (1888).

After graduation (1891), she studied music at Miss Burnham's Classical School for Girls (Northampton, Massachusetts, http:// en.wikipedia.org/wiki/Burnham_Classical_School_for_Girls), and entered Smith College (1892) where she studied art. Upon graduation (1896), she received further training at the Drexel Institute in Philadelphia and became an accomplished painter and illustrator for *Harper's* magazine.

As a Tonalist painter—a style that emphasized mood and shadow—De Cora often painted firelight in warm remembrance of her girlhood on the plains of Nebraska.

In keeping with President Grant's policy to bring Indians into the mainstream, she adapted to the two cultures and became the country's most widely known pre-WWI Native American artist, although few of her original works remain.

Rare for the era, her works depicted Native Americans clothed in contemporary mainstream garments. Her *Harper's* illustrations include *The Sick Child* and *The Grey Wolf's Daughter*, both in 1899. She also illustrated stories for children about Native Americans.

Although successful at *Harper's*, she remained torn between the two worlds and lamented that she could never escape the image of an example of successful assimilation or "Noble Savage." One of her mentors at *Harpers* stated, "Unfortunately she is a woman, and still more unfortunately, an American Indian."

In 1904, she met William Henry "Lone Star" Dietz. They married, and also collaborated on some of DeCora's illustrations. She became a teacher at Carlisle Indian School in 1906 and used art to instill within her students pride in their Native heritage. She also encouraged them to utilize their cultures in creating marketable art.

Her oil painting, *For an Indian School Exhibit,* for the Pan-American Exposition in Buffalo, New York, was an example of the mastery and emotive power of her work, but she did few illustrations after she began to teach at Carlisle. DeCora exhibited her work to both Native and non-Native audiences and tried to change mainstream stereotypical attitudes toward Native American Indians through her works.

Linda M. Waggoner, a relative of Angel DeCora, penned a biography of her titled, *Firelight: The Life of Angel DeCora, Winnebago Artist.*

67 VIRGINIA YAZZIE-BALLENGER: TRADITIONAL CLOTHING DESIGNER

- Elevates Navajo garments to wearable art

Award-winning fashion designer, Virginia Yazzie-Ballenger, was born in Lake Springs about fifteen miles southwest of Gallup, New Mexico. She is of the Meadow People Clan born for the Bitter Water Clan. She graduated from Gallup High School (1975), attended Loma Linda University in Riverside, California, and studied pattern making at Texas Women's University in Denton, Texas.

As a child, she cut models from catalogues and used them as paper dolls. They were her first toys, and her first experience with design was creating paper clothes for them. Her career as a designer resulted from her inability to find clothing that expressed her Native heritage.

A beauty in her own right, Yazzie-Ballenger was Miss Indian New Mexico (1982-83) and represented the company where she worked as Miss Santa Fe Railroad Safety Queen.

As she sought to represent her heritage better in the pageants and when she entered the work force, she discovered it was impossible to find traditional style clothing, so she decided to make her own. In doing so, she discovered she enjoyed creating and designing through the fabric medium.

Her skill in creating traditional works in velvet were inspired from memories of the old-style Navajo blouses and skirts her grandmother wore. She was also intrigued by old family photographs and historical styles that link Navajo history with the contemporary Southwest.

But even though she is motivated by them, Yazzie-Ballenger infuses her own ideas into the creation of new designs, and does so with a level of skill that elevates her garments to wearable art.

She has been a designer at her own company, Navajo Spirit Southwestern Wear since its launching in 1984, and her creations earned her a grant to study historical Indian garments at the Smithsonian in New York City. She was also awarded a Southwestern Association of Indian Arts (SWAIA) fellowship, an organization that produces the world-renowned Santa Fe Indian Market.

Navajo Spirit Southwestern Wear was featured in *Native Peoples* magazine (July-August 2000) and also in *New Mexico* magazine (2001).

Yazzie-Ballenger has shown her work at the Heard Museum in Phoenix; Red Earth exhibition in Oklahoma City; Gallup Ceremonial; Santa Fe Indian Market; and other venues.

Her honors include numerous Best of Class awards from competitions sponsored by the Indian Arts and Crafts Association, New Mexico State Fair, and other prestigious shows throughout the Southwest.

In February 2012, Bronitsky and Associates, specialists in working with and marketing Indigenous talent since 1992, produced a one-woman show for Virginia Yazzie-Ballenger in Moscow with the US Embassy.

Contact: fashions@navajospirit.com
www.bronitskyandassociates.com/wordpress/

68 MARIA MONTOYA MARTINEZ (1887-1980), POTTER

- Her blackware pottery skills preserved Pueblo People's legacy

Born in San Ildefonso Pueblo, New Mexico, Maria Antonia Montoya learned pottery skills as a youngster by observing her aunt. But it was a time of transition, when enamelware and Spanish tin ware were quickly making the creation of traditional serving pots less necessary. As a result, the techniques of creating traditional pottery was falling into extinction.

Maria and her family became involved in keeping the tradition alive when broken pieces of polished black-on-black pottery, a pre-historic style crafted by the Pueblo peoples, were unearthed in an ancient pueblo site near San Ildefonso during a 1908 to 1909 archaeological excavation led by Dr. Edgar Lee Hewett.

An archaeologist and anthropologist, Hewett focused on Native American communities (http://en.wikipedia.org/wiki/Native_Americans_in_the_United_States) of New Mexico and the southwestern United States. He identified the glossy shards with their melted appearance used only for decoration as crafted during the Neolithic period as described in *The Historical Pottery of the Pueblo Indians 1600-1800*.

At some point during the end of the eighteenth century, the glazed pottery became extinct, as finely powdered mineral substances and plant pigments became the favored method of painting.

To revive and preserve the ancient art form and place them in museums, Hewett searched for a skilled Pueblo potter to re-create the black-on-black pots. Maria Montoya, esteemed in the Tewa pueblo for her ability to make the thinnest pots in the least amount of time, was the perfect potter to make Hewett's idea a reality.

After a long process of trial-and-error experimentation that included figuring a way to dye New Mexico's red desert clay black, Montoya produced a rather rough quality undecorated, unsigned pot. A perfectionist, she was embarrassed and hid the pots away because her experiments failed to re-create the exact finish she had hoped for.

A few years later, Hewett returned to Tewa Pueblo and brought guests with him. They asked to see the pots, and to purchase blackware pottery similar to Maria Martinez's that was displayed in the museum.

Their interest spurred her to continue to experiment. With each pot, her proficiency increased. Collectors became excited, and a family industry grew out of their interest and demand for blackware pottery. She also began to experiment with other colorful pottery forms and techniques.

Her husband, Julian, mastered decorating Maria's pots, with many of his forms adopted from those on ancient Pueblo vessels: zigzags or kiva steps; roadrunner tracks, birds, feathers, rain, clouds, and mountains. The museum displayed the first two pots that he decorated.

Some of Maria's oldest works were unsigned, but over the years, she signed in several ways. Since dates were not added until recent years, it enabled collectors to approximate the times of her creations.

Maria and her family's gift to their people and to collectors worldwide is having resurrected a lost craft of the Pueblo people, and through fine artwork and craftsmanship, preserved it for generations to come.

---

69 Sharon Irla
(b. 1957), Artist

- Work described as "a combining of dramatic illumination and Old Masters techniques"

Sharon Irla is a self-taught, award-winning, Cherokee artist, enrolled in the Cherokee Nation of Oklahoma. She cites the techniques of the master, Caravaggio, for the development of her style. Her paintings of Indigenous women are so realistic they are frequently mistaken for photographs. Her work has been described as "a combining of dramatic illumination and Old Masters techniques."

Irla noticed that, historically, Native American Indian women have been subjects of art far less frequently than chiefs and warriors, and when they were, they were often romanticized, commercialized, or rendered with Euro-masculine features.

Her life-long observations combined to focus Irla's art on the remediation of Native American women's virtual invisibility and/or misrepresentations. They also forged an artistic mission from a Native woman's perspective to represent, through fine art oil paintings, traditional and contemporary Native women beyond the labels and stereotypes.

Irla's paintings do not neglect to depict the Native American Indian woman in her traditional strengths such as in the Council of Women, in which they once rendered important tribal decisions.

"Some, like Nanyehi (Nancy Ward), rose to the honored status of "Beloved Woman" or "War Woman," she states on her website. She laments that such women were seldom depicted in paintings.

Irla is also involved in preserving Cherokee culture through the arts, and is one of the founding members of the Southeastern Indian Artist's Association (formerly the Cherokee Artist's Association) which seeks to "advance the art of Southeastern Woodlands and protect the interests of Native American artists."

Through her involvement with CAA artists, she collaborated with a group of Cherokee artists, known as GaDuGi, which, in the Cherokee language, means working together in a community sense.

She assisted in the production of the outdoor art installment, *The Passage*, at Ross Landing, Chattanooga, Tennessee, where, she stated that many Cherokee were placed in stockades before being forced to walk the Trail of Tears to Indian Territory (Oklahoma).

Irla describes the experiences as "...an emotional journey home for all the artists working on the project."

In 2003, Irla began entering competitive art shows, and although most of her award-winning works are oil-on-canvas portraits of Indigenous women, her collective works include paintings, murals, graphics, photography, and custom picture frames with Southeastern Woodlands/Mississippian themes.

Seminole Smile (2012); *The Corn Mother* (2011); *Beloved Woman of the Cherokee* (2009); *Mississippian Ink* (2008); *Medicine Woman*; *She Was a Warrior* (both 2003); and *Aunt Jane Benge* (1999) are some of her historical figurative works.

Her contemporary figurative themes include: *Flowering Heart in the House of Song* (2013); *Save Xingu* (2013); *From the Garden Within* (2011); *Necessity Is the Mother* (2010); *Mother's Prayer* (2008); *Crows Stirring the Magic* (2008); and *Cherokee Beauty* (2007).

Included in her richly textured, mixed-media paintings are: *Tellico Mysteries* (2007); *The Bead Spitter* (2007); *Serpentine Birds* (2005) and *Ancestral Heritage I, II, III and IV* (2004).

Awards for her work, since 2003 include four Best of Show awards, and seventeen First Place awards, among others.

Visit Sharon's works at SharonIrla.com and other sites.

VI.
PHYSICIANS, NURSES, EDUCATORS AND PUBLIC SERVANTS

NO ONE STANDS TALLER THAN THOSE WHOSE LIVES are dedicated to the service of others.

---

70 SUSAN LAFLESCHE PICOTTE (1865-1915)

- First Native American female physician
- Founded first-ever privately funded hospital on an Indian reservation

Born in 1865 on the Omaha, Nebraska Reservation, Susan LaFlesche-Picotte was the daughter of Omaha Chief Joseph (Insta Maza, "Iron Eyes") LaFleche, last of the great Omaha chiefs, and Mary (One Woman) Gale.

LaFlesche attended school on the reservation, but because her father also believed in alliances with Euro-American reform groups, at age fourteen, she was sent to the Elizabeth Institute for Young Ladies in New Jersey. When she returned home at age seventeen, she taught for two years at the Quaker Mission School on her reservation.

But a childhood remembrance, that of a sick Indian woman who died because the local Euro-American physician refused to treat her, set her life on a different course. It reminded LaFlesche of the great need for medical care for her people and she decided instead on a career in medicine—an all but impossible dream for an American Indian woman of her day.

She returned East and enrolled at Hampton Normal and Agricultural Institute in Virginia. The school, which accepted both Native American Indian and African heritage students, was among the nation's first and finest schools available to non-white students of Susan LaFlesche's era. It would also set the stage for achieving a number of significant "firsts" during her lifetime.

When Martha Waldron, resident physician and a graduate of the Woman's Medical College of Pennsylvania noticed Susan's academic abilities, she realized her great potential. With Martha's help, Susan was able to secure a scholarship through the Connecticut Indian Association—a branch of the Women's National Indian Association—and the Bureau of Indian Affairs. The action made Susan the first person in the nation to receive federal aid for professional education.

She enrolled in the Woman's Medical College of Pennsylvania, completed the three-year program in only two years and, in 1889, graduated first in her class. After completing a one-year internship, LaFlesche became the nation's first female Native American Indian medical doctor.

Practicing largely as a Presbyterian medical missionary, she provided health care for approximately 1,200 of her Omaha people at the government boarding school. On 24-hour-call, she was known to leave a lamp burning in her window at night, so that those who needed her help could better find their way and know that they were welcome.

LaFlesche married Henry Picotte in 1894. They had two sons. They moved to Bancroft, Nebraska, where she began a private practice serving both non-Euro and Euro-American patients. When Henry was stricken with a terminal illness, she also tended him throughout his ordeal while rearing their sons and continuing her busy practice.

She was a community and church leader who advocated for public health, respect between races, and the rights of Native Indian people. In 1906, she led a delegation to Washington DC and won a battle to prohibit alcohol on the reservation.

In 1913 in the town of Walthill, she founded the first privately-funded hospital on an Indian reservation.

But Susan LaFlesche had health issues of her own. For about twenty years, she suffered from a degenerative bone disease that caused severe ear pain. Her health declined, and surgery to correct the problem was unsuccessful. She died in 1915 at fifty years of age.

After her death, the hospital she founded was renamed Susan LaFlesche Memorial Hospital in her honor. For more than thirty years, it served both Euro-American and Native American Indian patients. For an additional twenty years, it was an elder care center.

A local multiracial committee acquired the deteriorating property in 1988, and in 1989, it was listed on the National Register of Historic Places. Now owned by the Susan LaFleche-Picotte Center, Inc., a non-profit, tax-exempt corporation, it was declared a National Historic Landmark in 1993.

The committee's goal was to commemorate Dr. LaFleche-Picotte's example of student and servant as well as healer. It also sought to extol the cultural diversity of the people she served, and displayed both her work and the histories of the Omaha and Ho-Chunk/Winnebago tribes. A section of the museum is utilized as a childcare center and also provides support for troubled young people.

In 1992, Picotte Elementary School in Omaha, Nebraska, was named in her honor and in 2002, she was inducted into the International Women in Medicine Hall of Fame of the American Women's Medical Association.

Born during a time when racial and gender bias were instilled in public thought, Susan LaFleche-Picotte was indeed a woman far ahead of her time.

A version of this article by KB Schaller was published in Indian Life newspaper, March-April 2013.

71 ANNIE DODGE WAUNEKA (1910-1997), HEALTH CARE ADVOCATE

- First Native American winner of the Presidential Medal of Freedom

She was born in a traditional Navajo hogan near Sawmill, Arizona, to Henry Chee Dodge and K'eehanabah, his third wife, who left him before Annie was born. The infant remained with her for the first year and was then reared by Henry's first wife along with other half-siblings in a farmhouse rather than a hogan.

Compared to most Navajos of her time, Annie's was a privileged life where her father, a tribal council head, and his family enjoyed modern amenities on his large ranch. Once a government interpreter, he spoke fluent English and even had servants. But in spite of his comparatively upscale lifestyle, Henry Dodge did not want his children to grow up haughty and believing themselves superior to other Navajo children. He required them to herd sheep and perform other assigned chores.

In 1918 at age eight, Annie attended a government-run boarding school at Fort Defiance, Arizona. During her first year, the school suffered an influenza outbreak. After recovering from a mild case herself, Annie assisted the nurses with others who were ill. Little did she know that she had taken the first step onto what would become her life's path.

She was later sent to an Indian school in Albuquerque, New Mexico, where she met George Wauneka. Annie was never one to walk lock-step with the crowd, so, contrary to Navajo tradition that dictated family-arranged marriages, she chose her own mate. As a nineteen-year old 11th grader, in 1929, she left school to marry George.

During her school years, Henry Dodge was elected as first chairman of the Navajo Tribal Council and, in keeping with the rules of the Indian Reorganization Act of 1934, organized it to govern the tribe as a corporation.

As her father's aide, Annie often accompanied him to reservations while her husband, George, stayed at home with their six children and tended their properties and herds.

It was during such visits that Annie witnessed the ravages of disease, mainly tuberculosis. She knew that "white man's medicine" could hold the answer, and tried to encourage her people to practice sanitation in their cooking, eating areas, and food preparation. Because the community respected and trusted medicine men, she also attempted to recruit them as allies to assist in promoting modern health improvement methods.

After her father died (1946), Annie Wauneka became active in tribal politics and was elected to the Navajo Tribal Council (1951). She was only the second woman to be elected to the position (Lilakai Julian Neil was the first woman elected and served from 1946 to 1951). Wauneka served three consecutive terms and was also head of the Council's Health and Welfare Committee for twenty-seven years.

Utilizing her platform as tribal leader, her health education efforts regarding the prevention and treatment of disease saved many Navajo lives. Even so, to better herself and to render even greater services, in 1959, Wauneka returned to school and earned a bachelor's degree in public health from the University of Arizona.

Among her many tributes and honors, she received the Press Women's Association Woman of Achievement Award (1958); was named Outstanding Worker in Public Health of the Arizona Public Health Association (1959); and was also honored with an achievement award from the Grand Council Fire of American Indians of Chicago (1960).

In the same year, Wauneka was host of her own daily radio show in Gallup, New Mexico, which covered health concerns as well as items of general interest. She was also active in the Head Start program.

As Wauneka expanded her activities into both state and federal government, she served on the New Mexico Committee on Service to the Navajo. For her service, in 1963 President Lyndon B. Johnson awarded her the United States Presidential Medal of

Freedom for her untiring labor that "helped dramatically to lessen the menace of disease among her people and improve their way of life." She was the first Native American to receive the honor.

She was advisor to the Navajo Tribal Council into her 80s. In 1976, her alma mater, the University of Arizona, awarded her an honorary doctorate degree in public health. She was named Legendary Mother of the Navajo People (1984) and also received an honorary Doctor of Laws degree from the University of Arizona (1996).

Her influential study, "The Dilemma for Indian Women," was published in *Wassaja: A National Newspaper of Indian America* (September 1976).

When Annie Dodge Wauneka died in November 1997 after many decades of exemplary service to her people, Albert Hale, her grandson and Navajo tribal president, summed her extraordinary life best:

"She made us proud to be Navajo."

72 ELLA CARA DELORIA (1889-1971)
EDUCATOR, ANTHROPOLOGIST

- Was leading expert in traditional and Christianized Sioux culture

Ella Cara Deloria's Dakota name, Anpetu Waste Win, translates to Beautiful Day Woman. An ethnographer and linguist, she was born on the Yankton Sioux Reservation in South Dakota in 1889 to Mary Sully Bordeau-Deloria and Philip Deloria, members of a distinguished family. Her grandfather was a tribal leader, her father, the first Sioux Indian to be ordained a deacon in the Reservation's Episcopal Mission Church.

Reared on the Standing Rock Indian Reservation at Wakpala, Ella attended mission school and All Saints Boarding School in Sioux Falls.

After graduating, she attended Oberlin College (Ohio) in 1910, but transferred to Teachers College, Columbia University

(New York) in 1913, where she was awarded a scholarship. She graduated with a bachelor's degree in 1915.

Although Deloria was reared in the protestant Christian faith, she maintained strong ties to her traditional heritage, which contributed to her choice to become a teacher, and it was at Columbia Teachers College that she met and worked with Franz Boas. Initially, she served as his translator and field researcher in Dakota language and culture, but the preeminent anthropologist would also influence several of DeLoria's life choices.

In 1941, she collaborated with Boas in constructing Dakota Grammar, which still remains in use for the study of the Dakota language and is a primary linguistic resource. After Boas' death in 1942 and in 1948, that of Ruth Benedict, his student with whom Deloria had also worked, she produced and published previously unpublished manuscripts regarding the culture, language and storytelling of the Dakota people. It launched her as a leading expert in the field. Her recordings of the language are still highly regarded today.

Her writings include the nonfiction titles, *The Wohpe Festival: Being an All-Day Celebration, Consisting of Ceremonials, Games, Dances and Songs, in Honor of Wohpe, One of the Four Superior Gods ... Games, of Adornment and of Little Children* (1928); *The Sun Dance of the Oglala Sioux* (1928); *Speaking of Indians* (1944, reprinted 1998); and *Dakota Texts*.

Her fiction work, *Waterlily*, described the life of the title character and is considered Deloria's most extraordinary contribution to Native American Indian literature. It was not recognized or published until 1988 and was reprinted by the University of Nebraska Press (1990).

Her other fiction works were also published posthumously: *Ella Deloria's Iron Hawk*, edited by Julian Rice, University of New Mexico Press (1993); and *Ella Deloria's The Buffalo People* collection of stories, also edited by Julian Rice (1994).

She served her community as principal of St. Elizabeth School at Wakpala (1955-1958) and at the Sioux Indian Museum in Rapid City, South Dakota. She also lectured, gave demonstrations on

Native culture, taught dance and physical education, and worked for the YWCA and Camp Fire girls.

Ella Cara Deloria was fluent in, and had knowledge of both traditional and Christianized Sioux culture. A valuable community resource, she was compiling a Sioux dictionary at the time of her death, as, possibly, her last legacy to her people.

73 SUSIE WALKING BEAR YELLOWTAIL (1903-1981), FIRST NATIVE AMERICAN REGISTERED NURSE

- Elected to Nursing Hall of Fame

She was born on the Crow Indian Reservation near Pryor, Montana, to Walking Bear (Crow Tribe) and Jane White Horse (Sioux). When she graduated from Boston City Hospital School of Nursing (1923), Susie Walking Bear became the first American Indian graduate registered nurse.

Walking Bear returned to serve on the Crow Reservation and married Tom Yellowtail, a Crow religious leader (1929). She was appointed to Indian Health Services and worked in the Bureau of Indian Affairs (BIA) Hospital. Under the auspices of the US Public Health Service (1930-1960), Yellowtail traveled to reservations throughout the nation to assess and make recommendations for health, education, and social needs.

Among the atrocities she saw were forced sterilizations of Crow women without their consent. She also witnessed seriously ill Navajo children die on their mother's backs during the twenty-miles or more walk to the nearest hospital. It launched her on a life's mission to end such suffering and health care abuses.

Yellowtail joined state health advisory boards to fight gross inequities and before long, was known among healthcare policy-makers at the national levels. She was also a bridge between Indian and non-Indian people.

During the 1970s, Yellowtail was appointed to President

Richard Nixon's Council on Indian Health, Education and Welfare and the Federal Indian Health Advisory Committee. The appointments gained her a national platform to advocate for health care needs of Indian people.

Yellowtail founded the first professional association for Native American nurses and was instrumental in obtaining tribal and government funding to assist Native Americans in entering the nursing profession.

Among her many honors, she was presented the President's Award for Outstanding Nursing Health Care (1962); was director of the Montana Advisory Council on Vocational-technical Education; appointed to the President's Special Council on Aging; and was a board member of a number of other Indian-related agencies and associations.

Her photograph hangs in the State Capitol at Helena as one of Montana's most outstanding citizens. In 2000, the Franklin County Public Hospital Nurse's Alumnae Association proposed a commemorative postage stamp in her honor.

Besides their two daughters and one son, Yellowtail and her husband also had two adopted sons, a number of tribally adopted sons, and dozens of grandchildren and great-grandchildren.

Throughout her life, Susie Walking Bear Yellowtail maintained her Crow identity and heritage and was a talented craftsperson who created exquisite traditional Crow beadwork that she presented to family and friends.

She is listed in the Gallery of Outstanding Montanans, established in 1979 by the State Legislature and managed by the Montana Historical Society to honor its state's citizens who have made significant state or national contributions.

An outstanding Native leader, Susie Walking Bear Yellowtail challenged and surpassed obstacles of gender and race and took a stand for healthcare rights for Native American Indian people.

The Apache 8 Firefighters

- Women firefighter's team a "First"

For over 30 years (1974-2005), an all-female firefighting crew from the White Mountain Apache Tribe fought wildland fires in Arizona and throughout the United States. After 2005, men became part of the crew, but their presence did not make the story of these women, whose job sometimes required wielding chainsaws, cutting down trees, and thinning out areas, any less amazing.

The movie, *Apache 8*, explores their lives and the many challenges they faced told through four members of the team: Cheryl Bones, Katy Aday, Nina Quintero, and Ericka Hinton.

74 Cheryl Bones

As the tough and highly regarded crew boss who was responsible for their training, Bones led her team on firefighting assignments on and off the reservation. Although her leadership of the all-female crew sometimes earned her scrutiny and personal pain, as well as praise and respect, it did not dampen her pride in being a Fort Apache firefighter.

75 Katy Aday

In order to receive an education to help her people, Aday left the reservation as a child to live with a Mormon family. After graduating high school, she joined the military. She is a Desert Storm veteran and also became a social worker.

When Aday initially applied to become a firefighter, she was told by the director of forestry at the time that she was too small, and "couldn't do it."

She proved otherwise. In addition to continuing to fight fires, she also became a member of the board of education.

76 NINA QUINTERO

Not only does Nina Quintero fight fires, but also a personal battle against diabetes, a disease that menaces many Native American Indians. The dream of this long-time member of the firefighters is someday to become a crew boss like her mentor, Cheryl Bones.

77 ERICKA HINTON

The youngest member of the team, Ericka Hinton is a role model for the women of her age group and represents the future of female firefighters. One of the first women on the Apache Hotspot Team, she is dispatched to particularly active parts of fires.

In contrast to her other team members, Hinton fights fires alongside her husband. Both sacrifice long periods away from their children during fire season.

EXTRA: APACHE 8, THE MOVIE

In *Apache 8*, the female firefighters demonstrate strength, courage, determination, teamwork and leadership, but the film also depicts them in traditional roles—cooking, sharing personal struggles, and baring their feelings.

Each of them has earned national recognition for community or military service, but it was crew boss, Cheryl Bones, whose image is the model for the bronze statue at the Wildland Firefighters Monument that honors all firefighters.

Because the public has not always been accepting of women firefighters, the Apache 8 crew faced many challenges and their stories present yet another of the many facets of the lives of Native American women.

For more information: http://www.apache8.com.

A version of this article, "Apache 8 Female Firefighters Team a 'First', appeared as a blog: christianpost.com/bindings, August 14, 2012.

78 Doris Leader Charge (1930-2001), Language Instructor, Actress

- Dialect coach
- Portrayed "Pretty Shield" in *Dances With Wolves*

Born Doris Whiteface on the Rosebud Sioux reservation on May 4, 1930. Doris Leader Charge was reared in a Lakota-speaking home, did not learn English until she was sent to boarding school, and would eventually become one of only a few thousand Sioux still fluent in the language. She also taught Lakota language and culture at Sinte Gleska Community College on the reservation where her salary was $17,000.

Obstacles in her life were daunting. At age fourteen, she dropped out of school to help support her family. At sixteen, she married. At only twenty-one, she was widowed when her husband died of a heart attack, and she was left to support three children with another on the way, through whatever menial work she could find. At age twenty-seven, she married again, this time to Fred Leader Charge.

When *Dances with Wolves*, the 1990 multi-Oscar winning epic western film about a Union Army (http://en.wikipedia.org/wiki/Union_Army) lieutenant and his dealings with the Lakota Indians (http://en.wikipedia.org/wiki/Sioux_Indians) was still in the planning stage, Kevin Costner, director and star of the movie, also faced some challenges. In addition to his need to find enough Native American Indian extras for his scenes and 3500 buffalo, he needed a Lakota dialect coach fluent in the almost-lost language in order to achieve authenticity.

When someone recommended Doris Leader Charge—who had never seen or even knew what a movie script was—Costner sent it to her. In two weeks, she completed and delivered the translations to Costner. Her presence was commanding. And he recognized that fact immediately.

He also discovered that when some of the extras came late or had not studied their parts, he would need Leader Charge on hand at all times. To solve the dilemma, he and casting director, Elisabeth Leustig, offered her the speaking role of Chief Ten Bears' wife, Pretty Shield. She accepted the role.

During instruction sessions, Leader Charge used a hotel room as her classroom and proved to be true to her name—a leader who indeed took charge. A hard taskperson, she demanded perfection. Again and again, she required them to say their lines until they were flawless.

For her six-month experience with *Dances with Wolves*, Leader Charge earned $23,800. A practical woman, she used the windfall for practical things: repairs on her and her husband's $5,500 two-bedroom frame house. A new refrigerator and stove. And a washer and dryer.

She later stated, "I hope this film shows young people on our reservation, where self-esteem is low, that you have to do the best you can and be proud of yourself."

VII.
SCIENTISTS,
ENGINEERS,
MATHEMATICIANS

SCIENCE. TECHNOLOGY. ENGINEERING.
MATHEMATICS. THEY INCREASE OUR
UNDERSTANDING OF THE WORLD.

MASTERY IN THESE AREAS ALSO PREPARES THE
country's citizens to compete in a global economy, and keep our
nation prosperous and strong.

79 MARY GOLDA ROSS (1908-2008),
AEROSPACE PIONEER

- Only Native American female member of "think tank" to
  design concepts of a manned orbital space system.

Long before a man walked on the moon, Mary Golda Ross, the
great-great-granddaughter of Principal Chief John Ross (who
served the Cherokee from 1838 to 1866) was already experienc-
ing success in aerospace technology at Lockheed Missiles and
Space Company. She was its first female engineer. And the sole
Native American.

Mary was born in 1908 on her parents' allotment near Park Hill, a small Oklahoma town. Precocious and bright, she was sent to live with her grandparents in Tahlequah for better educational opportunities. She was taught the value of education in her early life and was reared realizing its importance for both genders.

At age sixteen, Mary enrolled in Northeastern State Teacher's College (Tahlequah), which Chief John Ross helped to found. She excelled in mathematics, chemistry, and physics. At age eighteen, Mary earned her bachelor's degree in mathematics, and after graduation, taught for nine years in Oklahoma high schools. She earned her master's degree at Colorado State Teachers College in 1938 and enthralled by astronomy, took every available class.

She later left for Washington DC to work for the Bureau of Indian Affairs (BIA). After World War II commenced, her father encouraged her to search for work in California, and in 1942, she was hired by Lockheed as an aerospace pioneer and mathematician.

Ten years later, as the only woman and the single Native American Indian, she became a member of a top-secret forty-member engineer "think tank" dubbed, "Lockheed Skunk Works." Its purpose was to design concepts of a manned orbital space system that could one day fly interplanetary missions to Mars and Venus.

Ross also worked on concepts of orbiting satellites for defense and civilian purposes and her work was said by the officials to be critical to America's Agena space rocket project.

Although she had always been proud of her heritage, hers was always a full schedule, so Ross did not own a single traditional Cherokee dress until she was 96 years of age. Fashioned by her niece, she wore it to the 2004 opening of the Smithsonian's new National Museum of the American Indian to which she left a generous bequest. She believed it important to perpetuate the museum's mission to preserve the education and culture of the American Indian.

"Just think, a Cherokee woman from Park Hill helped put an American on the moon."

—Cara Cowan Watts,
Tribal Councilwoman,
elected legislator at Cherokee Tribal Council

80 OTAKUYE CONROY-BEN, PHD (B. 1977), ENVIRONMENTAL ENGINEER

- First Lakota to earn doctorate degree in environmental engineering

The oldest of five children of Vina and Arlo Conroy, Otakuye Conroy-Ben (Oglala Sioux) is originally from Porcupine, South Dakota. Her Lakota name, Titakuye Ota Win (Many Relatives Woman), was given her by her grandmother.

Porcupine is a small Native American community located in Shannon County, the third poorest in the United States. It is where Dr. Conroy-Ben lived for the first five years of her life in a small one-room house that had electricity but no indoor plumbing. Her parents were among the roughly 80 percent on the Reservation who were unemployed, so they moved to Rapid City where both found work at Indian Health Services.

In spite of their circumstances, Vina and Arlo Conroy always valued and encouraged education for their children. Both had taken college courses, and although neither had earned an undergraduate degree, they knew that higher education would prepare their children for opportunities to succeed.

Always taught to be proud of her heritage, close cultural ties to Otakuye's community were forged at an early age when she began Fancy Shawl dancing at age four. As a teen, she developed a passion for acting and appeared in several American Indian-themed movies.

In *Dances with Wolves*, she played Kicking Bird's daughter. She was Mary in *Miracle in the Wilderness*, and an extra in both *Thunderheart* and *Lakota Woman*. She appeared in several local television and radio commercials and was a model for the calendar, *Runway Beauty Native America*. She also represented the Lakota of the Black Hills as He Sapa Win (Miss Black Hills Nation).

Always a "math whiz," Dr. Conroy-Ben graduated from Rapid City Central High School in 1994 and received a scholarship to Notre Dame. The pageants and her acting career were placed on hold. When she received her bachelor's degree in chemistry, she became the first in her family to earn an undergraduate degree. Her MA in analytical chemistry, MS and PhD in environmental engineering, were earned from the University of Arizona.

For her outstanding achievements as a PhD student, she received the University of Arizona's Centennial Achievement Graduate Award. The honor is given to students from groups that are traditionally underrepresented, have excelled academically, and contributed to their family and community.

The award included a $500 cash prize from the university's Division of Campus Life and the University of Arizona Graduate College. She also received an engraved plaque from the university's Alumni Association.

After completing a post-doctoral appointment in chemistry and biochemistry (also at the University of Arizona), Dr. Conroy-Ben accepted a tenure-track faculty position in the Department of Civil and Environmental Engineering at the University of Utah in Salt Lake City.

She is a registered professional engineer in the state of Utah, is one of only a handful of American Indian professors in engineering in the United States, and is believed to be the first Native American female engineering professor.

Dr. Conroy-Ben has worked on projects with chemical and environmental engineering professor, Robert Arnold. Her work is also part of a study to determine how wastewater can be recycled and reused to address future water shortages. Because the female hormone estrogen is found in both groundwater and soils affected by wastewater in degrees that can harm humans, her interest extends to future challenges of the regulation and removal of such from water supplies.

In 2009, she was elected secretary of the Board of Directors for the American Indian Science and Engineering Society (AISES). She is also a founding member of the Indigenous Women in Science Network, whose vision statement includes honoring the wisdom of the elders while integrating cultural values with science to achieve harmony and balance for all generations.

As a keynote speaker, Dr. Conroy-Ben has delivered presentations on a variety of subjects at venues that include the American Institute of Chemical Engineers Annual Conference; Stanford University; South Dakota School of Mines and Technology; and the American Indian Science and Engineering Society Region V.

She has been twice-featured in *Winds of Change*, an American Indian-published, nationally distributed, full-color magazine with a focus on educational and career advancement for Native peoples.

Dr. Otakuye Conroy-Ben is married to Colin Ben (Navajo), and they are the proud parents of a beautiful girl. They reside in Salt Lake City, Utah.

81 FREDA PORTER (1957), MATHEMATICIAN

- Founded UNC-Pembroke chapter of American Indian Science and Engineering Society (AISES)
- President and CEO of Porter Scientific, Inc.

Born and reared on a farm in the tiny North Carolina town of Lumberton, Lumbee tribal member Freda Porter's parents were tobacco sharecroppers. Her father observed that Freda was one who enjoyed using her natural mathematical and problem-solving abilities to ease the farm's workload as she assisted him in paying his workers.

The same love of numbers led her to earn a BS degree in applied mathematics (Pembroke State University, 1978). After her internship at IBM, she earned her master's degree in applied mathematics (North Carolina State University).

She married in the meantime, and while raising a family, commuted to Duke University where she earned a PhD in applied mathematics and computational sciences (1991). At the time, she was one of only ten Native American women to hold a PhD in mathematics, which she taught at Pembroke State University and the University of North Carolina-Chapel Hill.

Porter completed post-doctoral work in applications of mathematical models to the study of groundwater contamination, and earned Water Pollution Control System Operators Certification at North Carolina State University.

From 1994 to 1999 she was a member of the Mathematical Association of America's Committee of Minority Participation in Mathematics, and 1994 to 1995, was consultant to NASA-Langley Research Center.

In 1996, Porter was one of twenty contemporary minority women scientists profiled in the PBS documentary *Break Through: The Changing Face of Science in America*. She was appointed to a three-year term on the Board of Trustees, University of North Carolina at Pembroke (2004), and in 1991 founded the UNC-Pembroke chapter of the American Indian Science and Engineering Society (AISES).

For three years, she directed a University of North Carolina AISES-sponsored summer mathematics and science program for American Indian 9th graders.

Since 1997, Freda Porter has been president and CEO of Porter Scientific, Inc., (Pembroke, North Carolina), an environmental and information technology services firm.

VIII.
ACTRESSES, DIRECTORS, AND PRODUCERS

AN INCREASING NUMBER OF NATIVE AMERICAN women are amassing awards and recognitions both in front of and behind the camera.

82 TANTOO CARDINAL (B. 1950), ACTRESS, ACTIVIST

- Played "Black Shawl" in *Dances with Wolves*
- Appointed a member of the Order of Canada

Born Rose Marie Cardinal (Metis/Cree) in Anzac, Fort McMurray, Alberta, Canada, Tantoo Cardinal began her career in 1975 as a film and television actress in Canada and the United States.

She is probably best known for her 1990 role as Black Shawl in *Dances with Wolves*, which launched her to international fame.

Cardinal was a founding member of the Saskatchewan Native Theatre Company. For her 1986 performance in *Loyalties*, she was nominated for a best actress Genie Award at the American Indian Film Festival, and also the Alberta Motion Picture Industry.

She had roles in *Legends of the Fall* (1994) and in the same year, received a Best Actress award at the American Indian Film Festival for *Where the Rivers Flow North*. She also co-starred in the popular film, *Smoke Signals* (1998).

Tantoo Cardinal's stage credits include *All My Relations* at Edmonton's Catalyst Theatre (1980), for which she received the Elizabeth Sterling Haynes Best Actress Award.

She was appointed a member of the Order of Canada (2009). It is second only to the Order of Merit in recognition of outstanding or distinguished service by Canadians. It is also extended to others who have made a major difference to Canada through lifelong achievement and contributions in every field of endeavor. In addition, Cardinal holds honorary doctorate degrees from several universities.

Also an activist, she is not reticent to speak her mind. During a Racebending.com interview, she lamented racism, sexism, and the scarcity of industry funding. Investors, she adds, fear they will not recoup their investments in Native-themed, Native-directed productions presented from a Native perspective.

Others of her many roles include: *Running Brave* (1983); *War Party* (1988); *Black Robe* (1991); *Lakota Woman: Siege at Wounded Knee* (TV, 1994); *Tecumseh: The Last Warrior* (TV, 1995); *Dreamkeeper* (2003); and in 2007, *Native Spirit and the Sundance Way*.

Arguably the most recognized Native American actress in the world, Tantoo Cardinal continues to set high standards in her chosen craft.

---

83 IRENE BEDARD (B. 1967),
ACTRESS, SINGER

- Voice and model for animated movie, *Pocahontas*
- Named by *People Magazine*, "One of the World's Most Beautiful People"

Irene Bedard (Métis/Cree/Inuit) was born in Anchorage, Alaska (USA), and reared in its suburbs, where she was active in performing arts. She studied musical theater at the University of the Arts in Philadelphia and co-founded Chuka Likali Ensemble Theater in New York City. She began her acting career in 1994, and played a supporting role in the Disney adventure film, *Squanto: A Warrior's Tale.*

In 1995 *People* magazine chose Irene, whose Eskimo name Goodiarook means, "someone who dropped," as one of its 50 Most Beautiful People in the World.

Probably best known as the voice and model for the Disney animated film, *Pocahontas* (1995) and *Pocahontas II: Journey to the New World* (1998), she has many other roles to her credit.

In addition to her attractiveness, she was nominated for a Golden Globe Award for Best Performance by an Actress in a Mini-Series or Motion Picture Made for Television for her debut role in *Lakota Woman: Siege at Wounded Knee*, a Bronze Wrangler award for the same movie, as well as for *Two for Texas* (1995 and 1999). She received the American Indian LA Film and TV Award for Best Lead Actress in a Feature Film for *Greasewood Flat* (2004) and Best Dramatic Performance Vision Award for *Into the West* (2006).

Also a singer, Irene Bedard once performed in a band (1993-2003) with former husband, musician Denny Wilson, while she juggled acting and motherhood responsibilities to son, Quinn (b. 2003).

Although she plays Native American characters with great emotional depth and is proud of her heritage, according to a BiggestStars.com biography, Irene Bedard also longs for opportunities to expand her acting experiences through portraying characters that are not necessarily ethnically linked.

---

84 Georgina Lightning, Movie Director, Producer, Screenwriter, Actress

- First Native American woman to direct a full-length film
- Co-founder, Tribal Alliance Productions

Member of the Samson Band of the Hobbema Indian Reserve near Edmonton, Alberta, Georgina Lightning (Mushwatchees Cree) is an outspoken advocate for Native American causes and champions a broader awareness and appreciation by mainstream society of Native cultures.

An acting coach and actress as well as producer and director, she is also co-founder of Tribal Alliance Productions, which focuses on issues from a Native perspective.

In her directional debut film, *Older Than America* (official world premiere, 2008), Lightning's expertise was demonstrated in her story that deals with effects of the Indian boarding school experience on individuals within a Native community. The film garnered nearly two dozen awards.

When Lightning's own father, who'd had occasional violent outbursts, committed suicide when she was eighteen, she searched for reasons. The idea for the screenplay grew out of her quest for information on a childhood about which he had been strangely quiet. The film, which she wrote and in which she also starred, was a result of information she gleaned from other family members and friends who shared their experiences in Indian boarding schools.

When deeper investigation sent Lightning to the boarding school her father had attended, she was saddened by the number of tombstones behind it. The names etched on them were silent testimonies to the many young students who lay beneath them. The experience contained the seeds for Lightning's production.

Shot largely on the Fond du Lac (Minnesota) Indian Reservation, *Older Than America* also made Georgina Lightning the first Native American woman to direct a feature-length film. It won three Best Feature awards in a number of festival competitions.

She also acted in *Yellow Wooden Ring* (1998); had guest roles in episodes of *Walker, Texas Ranger* (1998-1999); *Pocahontas II: Journey to a New World* (1998); *Johnny Greyeyes* (2000); and *Dreamkeeper* (2003).

Lightning was co-producer of the movie, *Hanbleceya* (2005), in which a Native American teen is torn between his father's embracing of the Euro-American culture and his grandfather's adherence to his Native traditions and heritage.

Among her distinctions and accomplishments, *Filmmaker* magazine, in an annual survey, called Lightning one of 25 New

Faces of Independent Film (2007). She received the White House Project's Epic Award for Emerging Artist (2010).

As a longstanding advocate for the advancement of Native American Indians in the film industry, Georgina Lightning founded Native Media Network, which is committed to achieving that goal.

All three of her children, Crystle, Cody, and William Lightning are, or have previously been, actors as well.

EXTRA: THE CARLISLE INDIAN SCHOOL

The Carlisle Indian Industrial School was the first off-reservation Indian boarding school in the United States. It was established in Pennsylvania in 1879 by Army Captain Richard H. Pratt, whose motto was, "Kill the Indian and save the man."

To accomplish his goal, Native Indian children were uprooted from their homes and traditional cultures and placed within a "total immersion" Euro-American model, where their language and all other vestiges of their cultures were eradicated. Boys were schooled in vocational and agricultural proficiency and girls in domestics—skills that would prepare Native children for the lowest echelons of wage earning.

85 SHEILA TOUSEY (B. 1960), ACTRESS, PRODUCER, DANCER

- Winner, Best Supporting Actress Award

Born in Keshena, Wisconsin, Sheila May Tousey (Menominee/Stockbridge-Munsee) was reared on the Menominee and Stockbridge-Munsee Reservations. She began Indian dancing as a young child but did not perform on stage until she attended the University of New Mexico (Albuquerque).

Although her original plan was to enter law school to specialize in Indian law and federal contracts, she changed her major to English and also began to take courses in theater arts. After graduation, Tousey enrolled in the graduate acting program at

Tisch School of the Arts (TSOA, New York University), one of the nation's leading centers for scholarship, professional training, and research in media and performing arts.

Her first starring role was as Maggie EagleBear in Michael Apted's movie, *Thunderheart* (1992), followed by *Medicine River* (1993). She had recurring roles as Emma Leaphorn for the PBS series, *Mystery!* and in NBC's *Law and Order: Special Victims Unit* as Judge Danielle Larsen. Other roles include HBO's *Grand Avenue* (1996); *Song of Hiawatha* (1997); *Dreamkeeper* (2003), and *Coyote Waits*, also in 2003.

In the TNT epic mini-series, *Into the West* (2005), a Steven Spielberg-DreamWorks production, she played the older Thunderheart Woman and has acted in many other movie roles.

Tousey performed opposite Nick Nolte, Sean Penn, Cheech Marin, and Woody Harrelson in the Sam Shepard play, *The Late Henry Moss* (premiered September 24, 2001). She has also acted in other Broadway, off-Broadway and regional theatres across the United States.

In addition, multi-talented Sheila Tousey has performed with the American Indian Dance Theater; co-produced the Kate Montgomery film, *Christmas in the Clouds* (2001); and made her directorial debut in *Salvage* (2008), a Diane Glancy (Cherokee) suspense drama concerning the effects a deadly accident has on a hard-working family.

---

86 HEATHER RAE (B. 1966), FILM PRODUCER, MENTOR

- Academy Award nominee, Best Director
- Owns production company, Appaloosa Pictures

Heather Rae (Cherokee) was born in Venice, California, lived in Los Angeles until age sixteen, was reared in Idaho, and graduated from Evergreen State College (Olympia, Washington) with a degree in cinema and multicultural studies.

Rae has worked in the film industry since March 1992 and was director of the Native American Program for the Sundance Institute. She has mentored many Native American filmmakers and screenwriters (1995-2001), and through the Akatubi Entertainment Film and Music Program, has contributed to film and music programs throughout the West.

Rae directed the short documentary, *Birth Our Own* (1990) and *Trudell* (2000), which chronicled the life of poet, actor, musician and former political activist, John Trudell; the project was thirteen years in the making. It premiered at the Sundance Film Festival (2005) and screened worldwide at more than fifty film festivals.

Trudell garnered Special Jury Prize for Best Documentary at the Seattle International Film Festival, and Best Documentary Feature at the American Indian Film Festival.

First Circle, a documentary that centers on the foster care system and the struggle of families and children faced with drug abuse, premiered at the 2010 Woodstock Film Festival.

Other Rae independently produced films include *American Monster; A Thousand Guns; Naturally Native;* and *Smoke Signals.*

She also had acting roles in *Silent Tears* (1998); *Backroads* (2000); *Most Funniest* (2005); and *Disappearance* (2006).

Rae was appointed communications adjunct professor of Producing the Independent Film at Boise State, Idaho, in 2008, and also in 2008, was nominated for a Best Director Academy Award for her production, *Frozen River*. The film also won the Sundance Film Festival's Grand Jury Prize as well as two Independent Spirit awards and was acquired by Sony Pictures Classics.

Heather Rae's own production company, Appaloosa Pictures, focuses on documentaries and, because of her success with both mainstream and independent films, in 2009 Variety named Rae one of ten producers to watch.

Extra: Akatubi Film and Music Academy

"Young people cannot become what they cannot visualize," Paul W. Chavez has stated, and in 2002, as the executive director of the Owens Valley Career Development Center (OVCDC,

Bishop, California), Chavez teamed with Native professionals in the entertainment industry, Yvonne Russo, Johnny Guerrero, and Kimberly Norris-Guerrero, to create a digital film and music academy. The objective was to train underprivileged Native youths in filmmaking and music recording.

The result was Akatubi Film and Music Academy, which has trained numerous students to record songs and produce short films. Seven have earned film festival awards. Over ten percent of the academy's participants have been placed within their field of interest in the lucrative entertainment business.

True to Chavez's statement, the Academy has broadened the students' expectations and proven to be one of the most powerful preventers of negative activities among Native youths who are exposed to such in many of their communities.

IX.
MISS AMERICA, TWO MODELS, AND AN ENTREPRENEUR

WINNING THE TITLE OF MISS AMERICA IS THE dream of most young women. Many may also aspire to become models. Three Native American beauties have proven that these are not impossible dreams; their accomplishments should inspire others to pursue dreams of their own.

87 NORMA DESCYGNE SMALLWOOD (1909-1966)

- First Native American Miss America

In 1926, Norma Descygne Smallwood (Cherokee), a former Miss Tulsa, became the first Native American Indian to capture the coveted title of Miss America. Winner of both the bathers review and the evening gown contest, she was crowned winner of the pageant the following night.

Born in Tulsa, Oklahoma to Edward and Mahalia Robinette Smallwood, on her father's side, she also had a half-sister and half-brother.

Smallwood graduated high school at sixteen years of age and attended Oklahoma College for Women where she entered the

Miss America pageant, and where she was captain of her school's hockey team. Her hobbies included swimming, horseback riding, and dancing.

During the year of her reign, she was poster girl for Westinghouse Electric, Meadows Washing Machines, and many other companies. For her endorsements, Smallwood earned approximately $100,000 dollars—considered quite a sum in her era.

Twice married, her first was to Thomas Gilcrease (1928). She gave birth to a daughter, Des Cygne L'Amour Gilcrease (1929). The marriage ended in divorce in 1933.

Her second marriage was to George H. Bruce, President, Aladdin Petroleum.

After her reign, Smallwood lived a quiet life, devoting her time to charities through St. James Episcopal Church in Wichita.

Sources: Wikipedia; www.missamerica.org/our-miss-americas/1920/1926

88 RANDY'L HE-DOW TETON (B. 1976)

- Model for Sacagawea golden dollar coin
- Only living person whose image appears on American currency

It is the dream of many little girls to grow up to be models, to dress in cutting-edge fashions and strut down the runway. But how many aspire to sit for hours as the model for a historical figure on a coin?

Randy'L He-Dow Teton (Shoshone-Bannock/Cree) certainly never dreamed of being chosen as the depiction of legendary Sacagawea, guide and interpreter for the Lewis and Clark Expedition.

Teton was born in Southeastern Idaho in the Lincoln Creek district of the Fort Hall Reservation. Parents Randy Leo Teton and Bonnie C. Wuttunee-Wadsworth (Shoshone-Cree) are both members of the Shoshone-Bannock Tribe.

She is the second of five siblings. Her middle name (pronounced he-dough in the Shoshone language), means "meadowlark." Pronounced hi-though in the Bannock language, the translation shifts to "close to the ground."

In 1998 when Teton was a twenty-two-year-old student at the University of New Mexico, the US Mint invited internationally renowned Texas-born sculptor Glenna Goodacre to submit designs for the new Sacagawea dollar coin.

Because there are no portraits of Sacagawea in existence, Goodacre visited the Institute of American Indian Arts in Santa Fe, New Mexico and asked at the front desk if anyone knew of a young Shoshone woman she might contact.

It so happened that Teton's mother worked at the museum and showed the sculptor pictures of her three daughters. The same night, Goodacre contacted Randy'L.

The modeling session, difficult for Teton, lasted two hours on one afternoon, but it required her to hold poses for long periods of time without breathing, and to assume many different positions.

But Teton believes that, not only does the image represent Sacagawea herself, but expands to embrace the power, grace, and humility of all Native American women. She further believes that all women have the same dignity as depicted in the image on the golden dollar.

She earned her associate of fine arts degree in museum studies at the Institute of American Indian Arts and studied at Fort Lewis College (Durango, Colorado). She graduated from the University of New Mexico, Albuquerque, with a B.A. in art history and a minor in Native American studies (2000).

To promote the golden dollar coin and encourage Native American education, Teton toured the country extensively as a motivational speaker. She continues to bring attention to American Indian and Alaska Native issues and concerns through appearances as both the character, Sacagawea, and as herself, a public speaker.

Teton contributed to the Museum of Idaho's exhibit and lecture series, *Discovering Idaho—through the Lewis and Clark*

Expedition, by visiting schools as the voice of Sacagawea. She was selected as curator for the *Poha-Ha-Ba, Land of Healing Waters* exhibition in Lava Hot Springs, which recognized the Shoshone-Bannock Tribe's history and culture.

Her numerous awards and honors include appearing on the cover of *Native Peoples* millennium edition magazine. She was elected Miss Shoshone-Bannock, Fort Hall, Idaho; received a certificate of recognition from the New Mexico Commission on the Status of Women; and has been the honored guest at many regional and national events.

As the coin takes its place in history, Randy'L He-Dow Teton, who states that her desire is to "help educate the next generation," does so from a unique platform: she is the only living person whose image appears on American currency.

89 MARIAH MONIQUE WATCHMAN, MODEL (B. JULY 12, 1991)

- First Native American tribal contestant to compete on *America's Next Top Model* television show

Born in Missoula, Montana, Mariah Monique Watchman is an enrolled member of the Confederated Tribes of the Umatilla Indian Reservation. Her parents divorced when she was very young.

Because her father was in the Air Force, she lived for two years in Germany while a youngster. Although she has traveled broadly all of her life and accompanied her father to Washington DC, where he worked for the National Congress of American Indians, she has always spent time on the reservation.

She is a graduate of Nixyaawii Community High School in Pendleton, Oregon (2009), where she was a stellar basketball player.

Also a statuesque and striking beauty at 5 feet 10 inches tall, at age fifteen, Watchman signed with Image Modeling Development (IMD), a modeling and talent agency based in Medford, Oregon, that works internationally with every major fashion market. Although she is signed with New York-based Wilhelmina Models,

IMD continues to act as her "mother agency."

In a recent *Indian Country Today Media Network* interview, Watchman, by her own admission, likes being a groundbreaker, a first at doing things, and recently did just that when she became the first ever enrolled tribal member to compete on Tyra Banks' *America's Next Top Model* (ANTM) television show.

She also admitted that becoming the first tribal Native American model on ANTM was instrumental in motivating her to appear on the show.

But her success is not all about Watchman. She also wants to empower and open doors for other Native American Indian women and girls who aspire to pursue their dreams.

Watchman further views her modeling as an opportunity to demonstrate to most non-Indian people who know little about Native Americans how multifaceted Native peoples are. She even utilizes what some would interpret as stereotyping as an opportunity to advance in her career.

Once asked to portray Pocahontas, a historical figure most are familiar with, Watchman did not feel typecast. She used the experience as a bridge to build understanding between Native Americans, the mainstream, and other cultures.

Neither is she content to bask in her accomplishments. She plans a T-shirt clothing line of her own, N8TV, and to donate 10% of sales to organizations and charities of her choice.

Watchman also plans to initiate a workshop, *N8TV Game Changers*, and tour reservations across the country to empower and inspire other Native youths.

When eliminated from ANTM, Watchman took it in stride. She is already an established model who works for *Seventeen* magazine, *Delia's* teen fashion catalog, and *Nordstrom*.

Watchman has worked in New York, Miami, Los Angeles, Thailand, Hong Kong, and Peru. She is the subject of magazine articles, has participated in Miami Fashion Week, and over a score of other fashion shows.

She is eager to lend her name to ventures by other Native American entrepreneurs. She graces the cover of the debut issue of the upstart fashion magazine, *Native Max*, the brainchild of twenty-one-year-old Lakota Sioux Editor-in-Chief, Kelly Holmes.

Her national exposure on ANTM afforded Mariah Watchman the chance for greater recognition in the mainstream, as well as Indian America. The experience, she stated in her ANTM exit interview, should propel her toward her goal to become "the first Native American supermodel."

---

90 KELLY HOLMES, MAGAZINE ENTREPRENEUR

- Editor-in-Chief, first Native American fashion-based magazine

Lakota Sioux tribal member, Kelly Holmes, has resided in Denver, Colorado, since 2007, but grew up on the Cheyenne River Sioux Reservation in Eagle Butte, South Dakota. In a recent Indian Country Today Media Network (ICTM) interview, Holmes, editor-in-chief of her newly founded magazine, *Native Max*, says that it was in Denver that she developed her proficiencies as a model, hair stylist, fashion designer, and makeup artist.

Her skills are now applied in her newest entrepreneurial venture. Her fashion-based *Native Max* magazine also features Native American talent from a number of other industries: modeling, music, photography, health, and sports.

Another unique feature is Holmes' desire to connect with all of Native America, including both genders and all age groups. Gracing the cover of the first issue is Mariah Watchman, first tribal Native American to compete on *America's Next Top Model* television show.

Holmes' own modeling career began at age 16 when she was discovered at a Denver powwow. At the time, she lacked experience in the industry and found it difficult, she says, to find Native designers and photographers willing to work with her.

It was during this time when she was working on modeling assignments around Denver that she conceived the idea for *Native*

Max, and her industry skills provided the necessary know-how to launch the magazine. But even as she found her own niche, Holmes also seized the opportunity to do something to help other Indigenous heritage people. There was talk that others were planning magazines, so in order to be first, in 2007, she began to prepare in earnest. She invested one year in building the necessary networking relationships, while she saved enough money to launch her magazine.

Working alone was difficult, but things changed when she met Derek Nez (Navajo) at a Denver powwow. Initially, he was interested only in photographing her as a model, but soon became enthralled with the idea for the magazine, also.

At the same powwow, Holmes met Crystal Lee, also Navajo, recruited her as a model, and before long, the concept of the magazine captivated Lee, also. Holmes now considers both Nez and Lee partners, as well as co-editors.

Although the *Native Max* preview issue was digital, the premiere issue in August 2012 was a quarterly high-gloss print with high-definition photographs and high-quality ink.

Holmes has stated that she enjoys working with all Native peoples and eschews cliques. She also acknowledges that, although all Native American Indians are generally considered as one race, "we're all different."

For subscription information: native-max.com.

X.
MILITARY
AND OTHER
HEROINES

Native American Women Veterans:
Revolutionary War to World War II ...
and a Few Besides

"Native people are, in fact, defenders of two sovereigns—
their individual tribal nations and the United States of
America, with proud service to both."

—Roy Cook (Opata-Oodham),
Green Beret Special Forces Veteran

According to the Women in Military Service
For America Memorial Foundation, far too little is known about
the service of Native American women in the United States military. To fill the gap in information, the foundation encourages
Native American women veterans to register with the organization
so that they may be recognized for their contributions.

Although recent research has uncovered and verified some
who were cloaked by time, the information is still sparse. Included
here are the available biographical sketches of far too few women
of Indigenous heritage who served from the Revolutionary War
through WWII ... and one who served in Iraq and paid the ultimate price.

91 Pocahontas (ca. 1595-1617)
Colonial Figure, Peacemaker

• Brought food to starving colonists

Matoaka, born in Werowocomoco (weh-roh-wuh-KOH-muh-koh), Virginia earned the nickname "Pocahontas" as a child because of her playfulness.

Arguably the most famous of all historical Native American Indian women, she was the favorite daughter of Powhatan, head of a group of tribal Algonquin-speaking minor chiefdoms and groups. Her mother, whose name history did not record, was one of Powhatan's many wives.

Although the story of Pocahontas has been widely romanticized in art, literature, and film, in *A True Relation of Virginia*, Captain John Smith's 1608 accounts, he describes Pocahontas as a child of approximately ten years of age when they met in the spring of that year. Nowhere ever does Smith hint of any romantic relationship with her.

He does, however, describe the circumstances in which Pocahontas saved his life. As a captive in a longhouse, she placed her head upon his own when her father raised his club to execute him.

Her compassionate heart is further demonstrated when she brought food to the colonists when they were on the verge of starvation. Even so, during the 1613 Euro-Indian hostilities, Pocahontas was kidnapped by Captain Argall, whose intention was to trade her for concessions from Powhatan.

During this time, leading colonists worked diligently to convert Pocahontas to the Christian faith, and it was then that she and John Rolfe (not Captain John Smith), a tobacco planter, fell in love. She did become a Christian convert and was baptized as Rebecca.

She and John Rolfe were married in April 1614 and she became known as Lady Rebecca Rolfe. Theirs was the first recorded interracial marriage in American history. In January 1615, Pocahontas gave birth to a son, Thomas. The six years of peace that followed their marriage created between Powhatan's tribes and the Jamestown colonists what was called the "Peace of Pocahontas."

Pocahontas, John Rolfe, and their son traveled to London in 1616. By some accounts, she became something of a celebrity when presented to English society and also posed for a portrait. The inscription on the engraving reads: MATOAKA ALS REBECCA FILIA POTENTISS: PRINC: POWHATANI IMP:VIRGINIÆ (Matoaka, alias Rebecca, daughter of the most powerful prince of the Powhatan Empire of Virginia).

In March of 1617 when she and her family set sail to return home, Pocahontas became gravely ill, possibly from pneumonia or tuberculosis. The ship returned to land, and at age 21 or 22, Pocahontas—Lady Rebecca Rolfe—died in Gravesend, Kent, England and was buried there in Saint George Churchyard.

Her descendents through her son, Thomas, include Edith Wilson (wife of President Woodrow Wilson), Nancy Reagan (wife of President Ronald Reagan), and several other high profile personalities.

A number of cities and other sites in Virginia are named in her honor: a state park, a preschool and kindergarten, and a pancake house are among them, as well as Lake Matoaka Amphitheatre at the College of William & Mary.

Other places named for her include towns in Iowa, West Virginia, Arkansas, and Pennsylvania. A series of ships are also named in her honor.

92 TYONAJANEGEN

- Revolutionary War participant

According to an account in the September 3, 1777 *Pennsylvania Journal and Weekly Advertiser*, Tyonajanegen (Two Kettles Together), armed with two pistols, rode into battle alongside her husband, Hanyery Tehawenkaragwen (He Who Takes Up the Snow Shoe). He was a wealthy Oneida who owned his own farm, house, and livestock and was also a chief warrior of the Wolf Clan. Their son, Cornelius, rode with them.

When Hanyery was wounded in the wrist by a musket ball, Tyonajanegen reloaded his gun for him and enabled him to continue in battle.

After the August 6, 1777 Battle of Oriskany ended some six hours later, it was she who rode on horseback to bring the news of the outcome to local American rebels and other Native American Indians.

The newspaper account described Tyonajanegen and her family as "a friendly Indian with his wife and son." The article further lauded Hanyery as having killed nine of the enemy, described his wound, and how he had then used his tomahawk to fight when he was no longer able to use his firearm.

Cornelius is described as having killed two of the enemy, and Tyonajanegen as having fought with pistols by her husband's side. She is also said to have carried messages for the rebels.

Her actions and those of her family and other Oneidas were greater factors in the birth of the United States than any other colonial community of similar size.

93 Sacagawea (ca. 1788, ca. 1812), Explorer, Interpreter

- Her knowledge ensured the success of the Lewis and Clark Expedition
- Became Honorary Sergeant, Regular Army

Like Pocahontas, many myths have sprung up around Sacagawea (whose name means Boat Launcher or Bird Woman in the Shoshone and Hidatsa languages), but what is known about her is that her skills enabled the success of the Lewis and Clark Expedition.

There are several spellings of the name of the only woman on the expedition: Sacagawea, Sacajawea, Sakakawea. She was born in Lemhi County near present-day Salmon, Idaho, and was the daughter of a Shoshone chief.

When she was around age thirteen, the Hidatsa, enemies of the Shoshone, captured Sacagawea and several other Shoshone girls during a battle between the two tribal nations. Sacagawea was sold to French-Canadian trapper, Toussaint Charbonneau, and made one of his wives.

In November 1804 at the request of President Thomas Jefferson, Meriwether Lewis and William Clark began an expedition known as the Corps of Discovery to survey the land west of the Mississippi, which had been purchased from France in 1803. They also aimed to find a route to the Pacific Ocean.

Sacagawea and her husband had been living among the Hidatsa and Mandan (near present-day Washburn, North Dakota), when the Corps of Discovery built Fort Mandan. While they were there for the winter, they met Charbonneau and hired him as an interpreter of the Gros Ventre language.

Lewis noted in his journal that Sacagawea was pregnant with her first child at the time, and gave birth on February 11, 1805. Because the Corps needed someone to interpret and secure supplies when they passed through Shoshone territory, Sacagawea was also hired to accompany her husband, and when the journey commenced on April 7, 1805, she joined them, carrying her infant on a cradleboard.

As she traveled with her newborn, she was instrumental in gathering edible plants for the expedition. Later, when one of the boats capsized, Lewis further recorded that it was her quick actions, which saved important documents, medicine, and other merchandise. Lewis further wrote that about one week later, they discovered a beautiful river that they named Sacagawea River in her honor.

Also important to the expedition was the fact that as a woman with a child, she represented peace, which ensured that they were treated with less suspicion than if the group were comprised only of men.

The importance of her presence was further evident when the Corps encountered a group of Shoshone Indians led by, Sacagawea was to discover, her own brother, Cameahwait. The expedition was then able to purchase horses and supplies, and to hire guides to lead them.

They reached the Pacific coast in November 1805. Mission accomplished, the guides headed back, but Sacagawea remained with the expedition until they reached the Mandan villages. By then, William Clark had become so fond of baby Jean Baptiste, nicknamed "Pomp," he offered to finance his education.

Details of Sacagawea's life become more vague after the expedition, but many tributes have been paid to her over the years. During the early 20th century, the National American Woman Suffrage Association enhanced her popularity when they adopted her as their symbol to exemplify female worth and independence. They also erected several statues and plaques in her honor.

Sacagawea River, Lake Sakakawea, the USS Sacagawea, Mount Sacagawea, and Sacajawea Peak are all named in her honor. A huge caldera on the planet Venus, Sacajawea Patera, also bears her name.

In addition, although no extant images exist of her, in 2000, the US Mint issued a golden one-dollar coin to commemorate her. Modeled after the modern Shoshone-Bannock woman, Randy'L He-Dow Teton, it characterizes Sacagawea in a three-quarter profile with her son on her back.

In 2001, Sacajawea was conferred the title of Honorary Sergeant, Regular Army, by President Bill Clinton.

THE SPANISH-AMERICAN WAR NURSES:
94 ANNA PLEETS
95 JOSEPHINE TWO BEARS
96 SUSAN BORDEAUX
97 ELLA CLARKE

- All were members of the Lakota Tribe

In 1898 four Native American Catholic nuns, all members of the Lakota Tribe who were nurses from Fort Berthold, South Dakota, worked for the War Department during the Spanish-American War. They served under the founder of their order, fiery missionary, Father Francis M. Craft (1852-1920) of Mohawk descent.

Contracted by the Daughters of the American Revolution Hospital Corps, Mother Bridget (Anna) Pleets, Sister Joseph(ine) Two Bears, Mother Anthony (Susan) Bordeaux, and Sister Ella Clarke left the American Sisters of Fort Pierre (South Dakota) to serve in Camp Cuba Libre in Jacksonville, Florida.

From there they were sent to Camp Columbia in Havana, Cuba, where there was a high mortality rate from infectious disease. Because they were Native American Indians, it was assumed they had "expertise" in working under less than immaculate conditions. But it would be disease that would claim the life of Mother Anthony.

The soldiers loved the Native American nuns who put their own lives at risk to nurse them back to health. They mourned greatly the death of Mother Anthony, but some in administrative positions disliked the nuns, because they were not members of an "approved" order. Others still harbored lingering hatred against all Indians because of the Indian wars.

After Mother Anthony's death, it took Father Craft's insistence before she was buried with military honors. Even then, she was not buried in Arlington Cemetery (Virginia) along with other fallen soldiers. Instead, she was buried at Camp Egbert, Pinar del Rio, Cuba.

To this, Father Craft fired off a letter of protest to the State Department. Controversy grew. His religious order fell apart and the remaining nuns returned to the reservation and resumed their lives as laywomen.

Anna Pleets married Joe Dubray and worked as a midwife. She was given a military funeral after her death in 1948, but was buried at St. Peter's Cemetery in Fort Yates, North Dakota. To the end of her life, she treasured an apron upon which dying soldiers had written their names and addresses so that she could write to their relatives.

Ella Clarke married Joe Hodgkiss, and her last years were spent in the Old Soldiers Home in Hot Springs, South Dakota.

Josephine Two Bears remained in Cuba and ran an orphanage until 1901, and then returned to the United States. She married Joachim Hairychin, but died in childbirth in 1909.

Extra: Father Francis Craft

Father Francis M. Craft left the Episcopalian faith to become a Catholic convert. He joined the Jesuits briefly, but his volatile temperament placed him at continuing odds with the Catholic Church hierarchy throughout the time he worked to establish an order for American Indian women.

Previously injured during the Wounded Knee massacre of December 1890, he was possibly haunted by memories of the 500 US soldiers who killed 300 Minneconjou Ghost Dancers. Unwilling to compromise on matters that conflicted with the Catholic hierarchy, he was quick to fight if insulted or felt threatened, and was known to carry a gun.

In the end, it was his flash-fire temperament and refusal to give-and-take on matters of controversy that rendered him unable to garner enough support to fund his order.

The nuns returned to life on the reservation and Father Craft was accepted in a parish in Scranton, Pennsylvania, where he served until his death in 1920.

World War I Veterans

According to Women In Military Service For America Memorial Foundation, fourteen Native American women, members of the Army Nurse Corps, served during World War I. Two biographical sketches were available.

98 Cora E. Sinnard (1891-1919)

A member of the Oneida Nation, Sinnard graduated from the Episcopalian School of Nursing in Philadelphia, Pennsylvania. She served with a unit in France for eighteen months and was the only American Indian woman to serve overseas as a nurse in that conflict.

She was a graduate of the Carlisle Indian School and at the end of the war, was ward supervisor for Wood at Milwaukee and in several other VA hospitals.

After a funeral service, the Oneida Veterans of Foreign Wars (VFW) held military rites at the Episcopal Cemetery for the army nurse who, formerly from Oneida, died at a VA hospital in South Carolina following a lingering illness.

99 CHARLOTTE EDITH ANDERSON MONTURE (1890-1996)

- Canada's first Status Aboriginal woman to train and work as a nurse

The first Status Aboriginal Canadian woman to train and work as a nurse, Charlotte Edith Anderson (Upper Mohawk) was a descendent of the great Mohawk military and political leader, Joseph Brant, who was also a British ally.

Born on the Six Nations of the Grand River Reserve near Brantford, Ontario, she lived in an era when Canadian law, under the Federal Indian Act, restricted its Status Aboriginal peoples from pursuing higher education. Even so, Monture applied to nursing schools in Canada, but was not permitted to enroll because of racial discrimination.

She found the climate for nurses more hospitable in America and was accepted into the New Rochelle (New York) Nursing School. Among the first of her generation to leave the reserve to pursue a career, she graduated first in her class (1914), and lived and worked in New York City as a public health and school nurse.

When the United States entered World War I, she volunteered for duty as nursing sister with the American Expeditionary Forces Army Medical Corps and served in Vittel, France. She would later refer to the experience as "the adventure of a lifetime."

After her service ended (1919), she returned to the Six Nations Reserve, married, and reared a family. She continued to work as part-time nurse and midwife at Lady Willingdon Hospital on the Reserve until she retired (1955).

Charlotte Edith Anderson Monture died on the Six Nations Reserve in 1996, six days short of her 106th birthday.

World War II Veterans

The following servicewomen represent only a small percentage of the nearly 800 American Indian women who served in a variety of roles during WW II. Although classified as American Indian, the tribal affiliations are not always stated in Women in Military Service For America Memorial Foundation archives.

100 Elva Tapedo Wale

A Kiowa tribal member, Wale left her reservation in Oklahoma to join the Women's Army Corps (WAC) and worked on army air bases across the United States as an Air WAC.

101 Corporal Bernice (Firstshoot) Bailey

Born in Lodge Pole, Montana, Bailey joined the Women's Army Corps (WAC) in 1945 and served until 1948. After the war, she was sent to Wiesbaden, Germany, as part of the Army of Occupation.

102 Beatrice Coffey Thayer

She served in Germany as part of the Army of Occupation and remembered being assigned to KP along with German POWs, who were accompanied by armed guards. Thayer remained in the Army until the 1970s and witnessed the erection of the Berlin Wall.

103 ALIDA WHIPPLE FLETCHER

Fletcher joined the Army during World War II, was trained as a medical specialist and assigned to a hospital at Camp Stoneman (California). It was an army port of embarkation for the Pacific, and she was on duty the night two ships collided at a nearby ammunition dump. Approximately four hundred soldiers died, and many more were wounded.

104 1ST LIEUTENANT JULIA HELEN NASHANANY REEVES (1919-1998)

- After honorable discharge, she returned to active duty during the Korean War (or Conflict)

She was a member of the Potawatomie Indian Tribe in Crandon, Wisconsin, and completed her nurses training at the Philadelphia Hospital in Pennsylvania on a scholarship provided by the Daughters of the American Revolution.

After the bombing of the US naval station at Pearl Harbor by the Empire of Japan on December 7, 1941, Nashanany joined the Army Nurse Corps in January 1942. She served in the 52nd Evacuation Hospital unit, one of the first sent to New Caledonia in the Pacific.

For several weeks before the Normandy invasion, which began on June 6, 1944, she served aboard the Hospital Ship *Solace*, and the following year, on the 23rd Station Hospital in Norwich, England, until V-J day.

Following an honorable discharge, she returned to the United States. During the Korean War, she returned to active duty and was mobilized with the 804th Station Hospital in Battle Creek, Michigan. It was there that she met military officer, Joseph Reeves. They married, reared their four children, and retired in Suffolk, Virginia.

As a warrior for her country, the Potawatomie Indian Tribe awarded Nashanany the high honor of an eagle feather.

She is buried at Quantico National Cemetery, a military cemetery in Triangle, Virginia, for those who served in the United States Armed Forces.

105 Private Minnie Spotted-Wolf (1923-1988)

- First female American Indian to enlist in the Marine Corps Women's Reserve

An Oglala Sioux from the Pine Ridge, South Dakota Indian Reservation, Minnie Spotted-Wolf was just out of high school when she became the first female American Indian to enlist in the Marine Corps Women's Reserve. She served from 1943 to 1945.

Although at 5-foot-5 and only 95 pounds upon enlistment, she was already toughened by cutting fence posts, driving a two-ton truck, and breaking horses on her father's ranch. She found Marine boot camp "hard, but when it was over, I was proud of myself and all that I accomplished."

As a recruiting strategy and part of military public relations campaigns, Spotted-Wolf was featured in the four-page comic book, *One Little Indian*. After serving her country, she taught in reservation and other small schools in Montana for twenty-nine years.

106 Ola Mildred Rexroat (b. 1917), Member, Women's Air Force Service Pilots (WASPs)

- Recipient, Congressional Gold Medal

Shortly after graduating from high school, Ola Mildred Rexroat, an Oglala Sioux from the South Dakota Pine Ridge Indian reservation, joined the Women's Air Force Service Pilots (WASPs).

At the Texas Eagle Pass Army Air Base, she was given the fairly dangerous assignment of towing targets for aerial gunnery students. Intrigued by pilots flying airplanes, she, too, went on to earn her pilot's license.

When the war ended, Rexroat remained in the Air Force reserve for nearly ten additional years, serving as an air traffic controller and Air Force reserve officer.

According to the WINGS WASP website, in a resolution passed by the US Senate, Rexroat and nearly one thousand other WWII WASPs received the Congressional Gold Medal. One of the nation's highest civilians awards, it is conferred "in honor of outstanding service to the United States," Senator John Thune, R-S.D. who co-sponsored the Senate resolution, stated.

At age 96, Rexroat is the last surviving South Dakota WASP and is believed to be the only Native American female to have served as a WASP.

"The WASPs served our country with extraordinary bravery, even in the face of discrimination. Their service was essential to the war effort, and this recognition of their heroics is long overdue," Thune added.

Extra: The WASPs

Because their records were classified and archived for over thirty years, the WWII WASPs were left out of much of the documented history of World War II.

It was not until 1977 during the Carter administration that legislation was enacted making the WASPs part of the Air Force. Prior to then, they received no back pay or death insurance.

---

107 Laura Beltz Wright (1909-1996), Sharpshooter, Eskimo Scout

- Served in Scout's primary mission alongside men
- Delivered US mail by dog team

Born in Candle, Alaska Laura Beltz Wright was a member of the World War II Eskimo Scouts, also known as the Tundra Army and the Alaska Territorial Guard (ATG). The units were created in

1941 during WWII out of the United States' concern over enemy invasion of the territory of Alaska. They patrolled the Aleutian coastline and the tundra to defend Alaska and provide intelligence on any enemy operations. The Scouts also rescued downed US airmen.

Most women served as nurses at the field hospital in Kotzebue, but out of about twenty-seven female members of the ATG, Laura Beltz Wright operated quite outside the traditional female role of her time. Her pastor and friend of the family stated that her life was "more unbelievable than a novel."

The best sharpshooter in her company and the sister of Senator William Beltz, she hit the bull's eye forty-nine out of fifty times during a training drill and served in the Scouts' primary mission alongside the men.

Wright delivered US mail by dog team, was a midwife, conducted funerals, and was involved in other community activities. She was also chosen "Queen of Fairbanks" in a beauty contest.

She married John Allan Hagberg and the two operated a gold mine while raising their six children. They moved to Fairbanks so that the children could attend high school and one of their sons would become an airline vice president.

Hagberg died in 1948, and in 1951, Laura married Dallas A. Wright. They moved to Anchorage and opened a downtown parka shop, where Laura designed and patented Laura Wright Alaska Parkys.

Her designs won numerous awards, including Best Costume in a Miss Universe pageant. Some of her most notable clients include Elvis Presley, Willie Nelson, Ricky Nelson, Shirley Jones, and Burl Ives.

When she died in Anchorage, Alaska in 1996 at age 87, Wright's obituary described her as one whose "cheerful heart and home were always open," and "an inspiration to all who knew her."

Laura Wright Alaska Parkys is currently owned by her oldest granddaughter, Sheila Ezelle (BuyAlaska.com).

EXTRA: THE ESKIMO SCOUTS

Organized in response to attacks on United States soil in Hawaii and the occupation of parts of Alaska by Japan during World War II, the Eskimo Scouts were also known as the Alaska Territorial Guard (ATG). They were a military reserve force component of the US Army organized in 1942 by US Army Major Marvin "Muktuk" Marston and operated until 1947.

The scouts were comprised mostly of rural Alaskan Native residents. Women were among the first recruits for the newly formed Arctic armed force. Minimum official enrollment age was sixteen, but Scouts ranged from eighty years to (unofficially) as young as twelve. Women and sometimes children trained with rifles, served food, assisted with transportation and operated radios.

Experts at living through harsh weather conditions and using their surroundings to survive, Eskimo Scouts are the only members of the National Guard on continuous active duty mission. They currently patrol ice floes in the Bering Straits, monitor movements on the tundra, and perform Arctic search and rescue efforts.

It was not, however, until 1971 that women were officially allowed to join the Army National Guard. The first of its official Eskimo Scout women were trained at Camp Carroll at Fort Richardson, Alaska. By 1980, about sixty women were assigned to Eskimo Scout units throughout western Alaska.

But this proud tradition of service and remarkable era in US military history came to an end in 2000. The Pentagon decided to retrain and reorganize the Eskimo Scouts as infantry units with the possibility for worldwide combat deployment and reassigned the remaining Eskimo women to noncombat units.

Women had always been active in patrol missions but did not receive pay, benefits or recognition for their work until the later decades.

108 LORI ANN PIESTEWA (1979-2003), SPECIALIST, US ARMY

- Recipient, Purple Heart and Prisoner of War medal, made the ultimate sacrifice

She was born in Tuba City, Arizona on the Navajo Indian Reservation. A loose translation of her last name is "the people who live by the water." She served in the US Army from 2001 to 2003. Her father is Hopi, her mother, Mexican-American.

In the family's tradition of military service, Piestewa's paternal grandfather served in the US Army, Europe in World War II. Her father served in Viet Nam, as did—according to the Naval History and Heritage Command website—more than 42,000 other Native Americans, 90 percent of them volunteers.

But on March 23, 2003, Lori Ann Piestewa, mother of two, a quartermaster soldier of the 507th Army Maintenance Company and her comrades were traveling in Nasiriyah in southern Iraq. Their convoy was ambushed, her Humvee hit by a rocket-propelled grenade. She and her comrades were taken prisoner, and Piestewa later died from her wounds.

Although American Indian women serving in the US military traces back to the Revolutionary War, Specialist Lori Ann Piestewa was the first US female soldier killed in the Iraq war, and the first combat death, ever, of a Native American woman in US military history.

She was awarded the Prisoner of War Medal, the Purple Heart, and was promoted posthumously from private first class to specialist.

A version of this article, A Memorial Day "First": Lori Ann Piestewa, appeared as a blog by KB Schaller, christianpost.com/ bindings, May 30, 2011.

First Native American Women Color Guards:

109 Mitchelene BigMan
110 Julia Kelly
111 Sarah Kristine Baker

"To bring awareness of the many women veterans, especially Native women veterans. To honor those from the
past and who are currently serving."

Mission Statement, Posted on Website

At the Denver March Powwow of 2010, Camille Clairmont, a tribal elder, spotted a group of women dressed in beautifully crafted
jingle dresses in the patriotic colors, red, white, and blue, that
boldly displayed their branches of military service on their backs.

She wanted to know why they were not marching in the grand
entry along with the male color guards. Mitchelene BigMan, a
former US Army Sergeant First Class, responded that it was because they were not official color guards.

Clairmont's curiosity set into motion events that would change
color guard history. The women's jingle dresses—the metal cones
jingle as dancers dance—were designed by the women themselves, she would further discover. And, not satisfied with the
women veterans' acceptance that they were not official color
guards, Clairmont replied that the dresses "spoke for themselves."

Shored up by Clairmont's support, BigMan and her sister veterans decided they would indeed march in the procession. The
decision, however, did not sit well with the male color guards.
They could march, they conceded, but only if they went to the
very back of the color guard procession.

Although initially discouraged, the group, after thinking the
matter over, decided that it was really an honor to be last. After
all, they would be the last color guards the audience would see.

When they entered the arena, the audience witnessed, for the
first time ever, an all-female Native American color guard.

But their story was just beginning. From the Denver experience,

BigMan decided it was time to address the needs of contemporary American military women. Having served twenty-two years in the Army with two tours of duty in Iraq, she founded the non-profit organization, Native American Women Warriors (https://www.facebook.com/NativeAmericanWomenWarriors/info). The Native American female color guard is part of that organization and is now a familiar sight at powwows and in festivities all over the United States that honor Native veterans.

The group's leadership includes its founder, Mitchelene BigMan, President; Julia Kelly, former US Army Command Sergeant Major, Vice President; and Sarah Kristine Baker, former Marine Corps Sergeant, Secretary. The three represent the Navajo, Crow, and Northern Cheyenne tribal nations.

As their ranks and popularity grew, they served as color guards at the National Tribal Summit at the White House (December 2012) and the 30th Annual Gathering of the Nations powwow (January 2013), as well as at other events, and are a big hit wherever they appear.

The jewel in their crown, however, is that from an estimated 2,800 groups that applied, only sixty were chosen for the January 2013 Presidential Inaugural Parade. The Native American Women Warriors color guard was among them and proudly participated in the inaugural parade for the second term of Barak Obama, 44th President of the United States.

Watch the Women Warriors color guard on YouTube.

EXTRA: A CALL TO BE COMMEMORATED

Veterans who wish to share their service stories may contact the Women In Military Service For America Memorial Foundation, Dept. 560, Washington, DC 20042-0560; Phone: 703-533-1155, Toll Free: 800-222-2294 FAX: 703-931-4208. E-mail: hq@womensmemorial.org.

Of the thousands of Native American Indian and Native Alaskan women who have served in the military over time, only 111 of them have registered to date.

XI.

ATHLETES AND OLYMPIANS

MORE AND MORE ABORIGINAL HERITAGE WOMEN are making their presence known in athletics, an area where, traditionally, they have been greatly under-represented.

THE FORT SHAW 10 CHAMPIONSHIP BASKETBALL TEAM:

112 FLORA LUCERO
113 ROSE LAROSE
114 GENEVIEVE HEALY
115 BELLE JOHNSON (CAPTAIN)
116 GENIE BUTCH
117 EMMA SANSAVER
118 NETTIE WIRTH
119 KATIE SNELL
120 MINNIE BURTON
121 SARAH MITCHELL

- Played before thousands at 1904 St. Louis World's Fair

The girls from Fort Shaw, the small Montana "country" boarding school were undefeated. But for the world championship, their basketball team faced the tough, "big city" St. Louis All-Stars, also undefeated, in a best-of-three highly touted competitions.

Of itself, the Montana girls' unlikely advance to the finals was not the stuff of legends, except that they were Native American Indians from the off-reservation Fort Shaw Indian Boarding School. And in an era long before "political correctness," their opponents were Anglo-Americans.

Ages fifteen through nineteen, they hailed from seven tribes across Idaho and Montana (some of them not historically friendly toward one another). But on the Fort Shaw team, the Assiniboine, Lemhi Shoshone, Gros Ventre, Piegan, Chippewa-Cree, Chippewa, and Shoshone-Bannock proved that in team sports, one could set aside ancient tribal animosities to focus on the individual. And winning. They played the kind of full-court boys' rule basketball that had stunned all their previous opponents.

In the first face-off, they delivered the All Stars a crushing 24-2 loss. In Game Two, energized St. Louis' young women attempted an aggressive comeback. It was not enough. The Fort Shaw juggernauts defeated them again, this time by a score of 17-6 to claim the World Championship at the 1904 World's Fair.

Overall, the local Anglo community cheered Fort Shaw. The media's exploitation of race and ethnicities, however, fueled the kind of sensationalism that boosted game attendance—and, possibly, sold more papers.

News reporters sometimes referred to the Fort Shaw 10 by blood quantum: full-bloods, half-breeds. At least one headline pitted "White Girls Against Reds." But the mentally tough Fort Shaw team members kept their focus and answered insults with continued excellence on the basketball court.

The Fort Shaw 10 would soon go their separate ways to marry and live out their post-championship lives in anonymity. Rediscovered a century later, they are immortalized in the narrative, *Full-Court Quest*; the movie, *They Played for the World*; and in May 2004, through a monument at the entrance of the present-day Fort Shaw Elementary School.

A version of this article, They Stood Before Kings, appeared as a blog by KB Schaller, christianpost.com/bindings, January 13, 2012.

122 JOSEPHINE LANGLEY (BLACKFEET), ORGANIZER, FORT SHAW 10 BASKETBALL TEAM

- Introduced "basket ball" to Fort Shaw Indian Boarding School

William Winslow, MD, arrived at abandoned Fort Shaw (Montana) in April 1892 to start an Indian School. Physical culture classes were soon launched for the boys, and he dreamed of the same for the girls. In December 1895, Josephine "Josie" Langley provided hope that his dream would be realized.

An aspiring teacher and the school's Indian assistant, she was returning to Fort Shaw after an illness, and had already learned the exciting new sport of "basket ball"(invented by Dr. James Naismith, 1891) while at Carlisle Indian School. When Winslow asked her to teach the girls' physical culture class, Langley seized the opportunity to introduce it into the curriculum while gaining teaching experience.

The school's budget had no funds for a pair of baskets and a regulation ball, so she borrowed a soccer ball from the boys' classes. While awaiting her equipment, Langley taught the basics. She drilled them in passes, deflecting or intercepting opponents' passes, and bouncing—or dribbling.

After six years at Fort Shaw, however, Dr. Winslow moved on, and it would be under superintendent, Fred C. Campbell that Fort Shaw would evolve into the most powerful girls' team of the era. By 1897, it was the only Montana school—Indian or non-Indian—to add basketball to its physical culture curriculum.

EXTRA: THE FORT SHAW TEAM MONUMENT

The monument to the World's Greatest Girls Basketball Team of 1904 is located approximately twenty miles west of Great Falls via Montana Highway 200, a half-mile northwest of town next to the elementary school. Source: RoadsideAmerica.com.

123 Sharon Firth
124 Shirley Firth
Twin Olympic Skiers (b. 1953)

- Both sisters inducted into Canadian Ski Hall of Fame
- Received the Order of Canada for their outstanding contributions to society

Aboriginal heritage twin sisters Sharon and Shirley Firth (Gwich'in Nation) were born in Aklavik, Northwest Territories, Canada, where along with eleven other siblings, their home was a log house in a traditional rural First Nation community.

When the twins were in their teens, due to severe flooding and erosion, the government required their community to relocate to Inuvik, a prefabricated township north of the Arctic Circle, one of the harshest and coldest climates in the world.

The sisters discovered skiing through a program introduced by a Roman Catholic French missionary priest, Father Jean Marie Mouchet, who had served ski troops during World War II. He had requested government funding for his fledgling ski clinic, the Territorial Experimental Ski Training program (TEST) for Canada's First Nations and Inuit people that would also teach leadership skills to Inuit youths. The Canadian government granted his request.

At once, Father Mouchet noticed the Firth twins' aptitude, eagerness to learn, and determination. They were also toughened by survival skills taught them by their father, a Loucheaux-Metis trapper. The girls utilized those abilities as they trained outside in the minus forty degree winter temperatures of the Arctic winters twenty-four hours of darkness.

During the summers, Sharon and Shirley ran long distances to keep fit, and over the years, increased in strength, skill, endurance and dedication that would propel them to the elite status of Olympic athletes.

For seventeen consecutive years, the trailblazing skiers were part of Canada's national cross-country team. In a variety of

World Cup circuit competitions, the Firth twins won a total of seventy-nine national championship medals.

The sisters were among the first Aboriginals to represent Canada at the Olympics, and the only Canadian women to compete in four consecutive Olympic Winter Games: Sapporo, Japan (1972); Innsbruck, Austria (1976); Lake Placid, New York USA (1980); and Sarajevo, Yugoslavia (1984).

They were also the first Nordic skiers to win the John Semmelink Memorial Award by the Canadian Ski Association for contributions to skiing in Canada.

In 1975 Sharon Firth became the first Canadian woman to sweep by winning Gold in the 5km, 10km and the 3x5km relay at the North American Championships.

Ski Racing magazine voted Shirley Firth Canadian Women's Nordic Skier of the Year six times. After her marriage, she moved to Europe and lived there for more than twenty years before she returned to Yellowknife, Northwest Territories.

In 1987 a few years following their retirement, Shirley and Sharon Firth received the Order of Canada for their outstanding contributions to society. Their story has been the subject of *The Olympians*, *The Firth Sisters*, and other documentaries. Both Sharon and Shirley Firth were inducted into the Canadian Ski Hall of Fame (1990).

They received the Queen's Golden Jubilee Medal in 2002 and in 2005, the National Aboriginal Achievement Award.

---

125 TAI BABILONIA (HOPI, MULTI-RACIAL, B. 1959) CHAMPION FIGURE SKATER, OLYMPIAN

- Olympic skater honored for charitable support
- Inducted into United States Figure Skating Hall of Fame

Tai Reina Babilonia (Hopi/multiracial descent) was born in Los Angeles, California. At age six, she watched a performance of Olympic Gold Medalist, Peggy Fleming, and became fascinated with figure skating.

At age ten, Tai met Randy Gardner who had already performed in many competitions and the two became skating partners. In 1973, they won as National Junior Pairs Champions and were the youngest ever to represent the United States at the 1974 World Championships.

Their first Olympic competition (1976) was in Innsbruck, Austria, where sixteen-year-old Tai and partner, Randy, finished fifth. Three years later, in Vienna, Austria, Babilonia and Gardner became the first Americans in a quarter of a century to win the World Champions competition and were favorites when they entered the 1980 Olympic games in Lake Placid, New York.

Randy, however, had suffered a groin injury, and although he made a gallant attempt to compete, the pain was too great. Both suffered a fall, and before a stunned world viewership of millions, the pair had to withdraw.

Although Olympic Gold eluded them, they went on to perform with Ice Capades a few months later and were among the first to receive an Olympic Spirit award.

They starred in the first ever ice-skating home video, *How to Ice Skate*, and in the landmark production, *Festival on Ice* (1988).

The television movie, *On Thin Ice* (1991) chronicled Babilonia's rise to the threshold of greatness, her descent into depression and alcohol abuse—and her triumphant return to the ice.

Babilonia and Gardner were inducted into the United States Figure Skating Hall of Fame (1992). Also of Filipino and African-American heritage, in 2002 the *International Figure Skating* magazine chose Babilonia as one of the ten Most Beautiful People in Skating.

She married Cary Butler in 1991. They divorced in 1997. The couple had one son, Scout Gabriel Butler, (b.1995). In March 2011, she married David Brenner.

Tai Babilonia has been honored for her support of inner-city children, children stricken with AIDs, and other charities.

126 ALVINA BEGAY, ELITE RUNNER (B. 1980)

- Four-time track state champion in 1500m and 3200m
- Nike N7 ambassador

The eldest of five children, Alvina Begay was born on the Navajo Indian Reservation to Alvin and Wanda Begay in Ganado, Arizona. She learned responsibility early. While her mother worked full-time, she cared for her younger siblings.

She used her "down time" running across the mesas and trails of Ganado, while she nurtured a goal to one day qualify for the Olympic trials. For a dream of that scope, she kept her mind, body, and emotions in top condition.

In junior high and high school, Begay lettered in track and cross-country. She was two-time cross-country state champion and four-time track state champion in the 1500m and 3200m among other achievements. During college, she continued to excel in the sport.

After Begay graduated with a bachelor of science degree in nutrition (2003), she put her pursuit of a master's degree on hold to focus on training for the Olympic trials. Her discipline and performance earned her that right—an accomplishment in itself as she competed against the best runners in the world for a spot on Team USA. She accomplished a respectable finish.

As a Nike N7 ambassador, she established a platform to encourage other Native American Indians to achieve and maintain physical fitness that can help to address the epidemic of diabetes and other lifestyle-linked, preventable diseases in Indian country.

Alvina Begay also set an example of establishing goals and of perseverance in the pursuit of them.

EXTRA: FIRST NIKE N7 NATIVE SUMMIT

The First Nike N7 Sport Summit for Native American and Aboriginal youth recreation leaders took place on October 28 through 30, 2011. More than four hundred attendees from the United States and Canada convened at the Nike World Headquarters, Beaverton, Oregon.

The summit delivered interactive sessions to educate, empower, and encourage participants to create sustainable sports programs that encourage physical activity for Native American and Aboriginal youths.

Alvina Begay kicked-off the second morning of the Summit with a two-mile walk/run around the Nike campus. She was also a panelist who shared how access to sports has influenced her successes.

127 MARY SPENCER (B. 1984), OLYMPIAN, CANADIAN FIRST NATION BOXER

- Was top ranked middleweight fighter in the world

As women's boxing made its debut at the 2012 Olympiad, Mary Spencer, Canadian First Nation Ojibwe pugilist, earned a berth on Team Canada as a Wild Card. When she began boxing in 2002 at age seventeen, her goal was to keep in shape after her basketball season ended. Instead, she fell in love with the sport and never looked back.

Her trainer, Charlie Stewart, is a three-time Olympic coach at the Windsor Amateur Boxing Club in Ontario, Canada. Spencer, herself, was eight-time National Champion, five-time Pan-American champion, and three-time World Champion.

Although in her middleweight class she was the top-ranked fighter in the world, Spencer lost at the 2012 world championships held in China. Several agonizing weeks later, she learned that she was one of four boxers in her twelve-boxers weight class to receive an opening-round bye with the opportunity to earn a medal. She fell short, this time, finishing in fifth place as a light heavyweight.

She is a member of Motivate Canada's GEN7 Aboriginal Role Model Initiative, which encourages physical activity and sports, and the empowerment of Aboriginal youth in First Nation Ontario communities.

Photogenic and attractive, Mary Spencer is also an ambassador for CoverGirl cosmetics.

128 MARY KILLMAN (B. 1991)
OLYMPIAN, SYNCHRONIZED SWIMMER

- Silver Medalist, Pan American Games

Born in Ada, Oklahoma Mary Killman is a member of Oklahoma's Citizen Potawatomi Nation. She and her partner, Mariya Korolvea, competed in the duet competition and were the USA synchronized swimmers to compete in London.

Although the two had been partners only since August 2011, they won a silver medal at the Pan American Games in Mexico in October 2011. They placed seventh at the Olympic qualifying meet.

Once a competitive swimmer, Killman gave it up at age fifteen to concentrate on synchronized swimming.

129 TUMUAIALII (TUMUA) ANAE
(B. 1988), OLYMPIAN, GOALIE, USA WATER POLO

- Team member, 2010 NCAA Champions

Tumua Anae is a Native Hawaiian whose grandfather emigrated from Samoa in the 1920s. She attended the University of Southern California as a broadcast journalism major and was also goalie for the women's water polo team her entire four-year college career.

After her senior year, Anae trained with the National team, proved to be a formidable force in the water, and has been on the American women's water polo team since 2010.

Anae was a member of the University of Southern California

women's team that won the 2010 NCAA Championship. She was also a force in the United States' Gold Medal victory at the Pan American Games. It guaranteed the squad a berth on the 2012 Olympic team where eight nations competed in women's water polo.

Also in 2010, she was a finalist for the Peter J. Cutino Award, and was NCAA Champion.

She made seven saves at the Pan American games (2011) and won gold in the FINA World League Super Final (also 2011) among other victories.

Tumua Anae was TEAM USA's 2012 Olympic choice as back-up goalie to Betsey Armstrong, named the world's greatest female water polo player.

130 Adrienne Lyle (b. 1985), Olympian, USA Dressage Rider

- Placed Fourth, US Equestrian Federation Dressage Festival

Cherokee Nation citizen, Adrienne Lyle, is among the younger riders in the sport. A 2012 first time Olympian, she was born and reared of modest means on Whidbey Island, Washington, on a small cattle ranch.

In 2005, Lyle worked part-time with highly successful dressage rider, Debbie McDonald, at Peggy and Parry Thomas' River Grove Farm (Idaho), and in 2006, was fulltime assistant trainer. In 2009, she and Wizard, a thirteen-year-old Oldenburg gelding by Weltmeyer, competed in their first Grand Prix.

Her expertise in the sport that involves a rider's guiding a horse by slight movements of the hands, weight, and feet through a series of complex maneuvers, won her an Olympic spot. Adrienne Lyle and Wizard placed an impressive Fourth Place in the US Equestrian Federation Dressage Festival of Champions and the USEF Dressage Olympic Selection Trials.

131 NAOMI LANG (B. 1978), ICE DANCER, OLYMPIAN

- Five-time US National Champion

Karuk tribal member Naomi Lang was born in Arcata, California, to Jason Lang (Karuk) and Leslie Dixon (French/English/Irish heritage).

At age three, Naomi began her ballet training in California at the Redwood Concert Ballet and at age six, performed as a bon-bon in her first ballet, the Nutcracker.

When she was eight her maternal grandmother became ill and Naomi and her mother moved to Allegan, Michigan to be near her. At the same age, Naomi became interested in ice skating after watching the Ice Capades, and attended her first lesson in Kalamazoo. She performed with the Grand Rapids Ballet Company and in many on-stage productions, while she continued her ballet training through age fifteen.

She and first partner, John Lee, won their first competition at the novice ice skating level. At ages sixteen through seventeen, they competed at the junior level where their highest achievement was second place.

The pair split at age eighteen and Lang's next partner was Russian-born dancer, Peter Tchernyshev, and the pair became renowned for their on-ice romantic performances. They trained with world-renowned ice dancing and skating coaches, Igor Shpilband, Elizabeth Coates, Alexander Zhulin, Nikolai Morozov, Natalia Dubova, and Tatiana Tarosova.

After turning professional, Naomi performed with many skating shows and tours, including *Champions on Ice* (2002-2003), and *Art on Ice* television shows. She performed live to artists including Earth, Wind & Fire; Michael Bolton; Frankie Valle; Robin Gibb; and others. She also performed in many Dission skating productions, was part of the Pandora NBC's *Skating Series*, and has traveled extensively over Europe with Evgeny Plushenko's Stradivarius Violin Tour.

Lang is a five-time National Ice Dance champion, five-time world competitor, and an Olympic team member (2002). She has won medals at five Four Continents championships and received the bronze medal at the Skate America championships (2000). She was the Junior National Ice Dance silver medalist (1996) and the Novice Ice Dance National Champion (1995). Naomi also won gold medals in Ice Dance and Freedance, and silver medals in Freestyle and Moves in the Field.

Following a 2004 re-injury of her Achilles tendon, Naomi Lang and Peter Tchernyshev retired from competitive skating, but continued to skate together in US ice shows. They toured extensively in Europe and Russia. The pair also performed in *Art on Ice*; *Kings on Ice*; the *Katarina Witt Farewell Tour*; and other shows.

Naomi Lang and Peter Tchernyshev have entertained celebrities including Brooke Shields, Katie Holmes and Tom Cruise, Jim Carrey, and Morgan Freeman. Lang's profile appears in Vincent Schilling's *Native Athletes in Action*.

Now an instructor in the Polar Ice Gilbert figure skating program, Lang specializes in ice dance, choreography, polishing of programs, stroking techniques, and freestyle.

A number of her students have competed at the junior national, national, and international levels.

---

132 Shoni Schimmel (b. 1992), Basketball Juggernaut

- Skills compared to those of "Pistol" Pete Maravich and Lebron James

Shoni Schimmel (Confederated Tribes of the Umatilla Indian Reservation, Oregon) has credited her competitive spirit to playing nightly games on the Reservation with her older brother and friends.

She played her first two years of basketball at Hamilton High School, and her junior and senior years at Franklin High School (Portland, Oregon). Schimmel earned First Team All-State and

First Team All-Conference honors throughout her high school career. She was named Oregon 5A Player of the Year for her freshman and sophomore seasons, and Oregon 6A Player of the Year her junior season.

Her record was so impressive, even though she injured her ankle and was forced to miss thirteen games during her junior year, she ended her senior year with 2,120 points. It ranked her sixth on the all-time list. During her senior year, she scored 805 points, the third highest single season total ever in Oregon.

Schimmel was selected to the WBCA All American Team (2010). She was ranked No. 8 player in the nation by ESPN's women's basketball ranking system, HoopGurlz, and third best point guard in the class of 2010. She was also named a first team Parade All-American.

When she began her first season (2010-2011) for the University of Louisville Cardinals, the 5-foot-10 point guard promptly added even more impressive accomplishments to her resume: starting point guard in all thirty-five games for the Cardinals. She was named a first team Full Court Press Freshman, and was the unanimous selection to the Big East All-Freshman Team.

Schimmel was also named Big East Freshman of the Week four times in one season. When she scored double digits for the eighteenth straight game, she broke the longest streak by a University of Louisville freshman that had stood for twenty years.

Her ball-handling, no-look-behind-the-back passes and deep three-pointer shots have been compared to those of basketball legends "Pistol" Pete Maravich and LeBron James.

In an *Oregonian* interview, Schimmel negates the widely-held notion by many NCAA programs that Native American athletes become homesick, return to their people, and will not work toward success: "I'm going to do my best to prove to Native Americans that they can do it, they can leave home and be Okay," she states.

Her phenomenal successes and role model status for other Native American young women are subject of the documentary film, *Off the Rez*, (Jonathan Hock, director; Kelly Ripa and Mark

Consuelos, producers). Its world premiere was on April 26, 2011 at the Tribeca Film Festival.

Shoni Schimmel was also part of a five-person White House panel that celebrated forty years of opportunities afforded girls and women in athletics through Title IX. Schimmel spoke on the positive impact of the 1972 Education Act, which stated that no person could be denied benefits of a federally funded educational program or activity based on their gender.

---

133 ALEXANDREA SCHULTE (B. 1988), PROFESSIONAL GOLFER

• Qualified for four LPGA Tours

"She represents the core values of our youth in the Native American community."

—Louis J. Manuel, Jr.,
Tribal Chairman

She was born in Houston, Texas, to Robert and Teresa Schulte. Her mother is a full-blooded Northern Ute tribal member. When her family moved to Broken Arrow, Alexandrea attended Bishop Kelly High School, where she won three high school golf championships. Among her wins in other competitions around the nation is the Oklahoma Junior Girls championship.

At age fourteen, the American Junior Golf Association named Schulte one of the top fifty teenage players in the nation. Upon graduation, she attended the University of Arkansas on a full golf scholarship, and was a four-year starter.

As part of the Arkansas team, her record includes four NCAA regional appearances and one in the NCAA Championship. She was awarded two Arkansas State Women's Amateur titles.

An *Indian Country Today* sports section states that her 2012 tour lineup included four LPGA Tour qualifiers; ten LPGA Futures Tour events; five Cactus Tour events that include the Florida Women's Open, and seven SunCoast Ladies Series events. Her Top 20 finishes in three 2012 tournaments include a Second

Place at the Cactus Tour in Phoenix.

Because of her record and high profile, Schulte has become "the face" of the Ak-Chin Community's athletic efforts. She is associated with the tribally-owned enterprise, Southern Dunes Golf Club in Maricopa, Arizona, and was a feature at the grand opening of the Ak-Chin Family Entertainment Center, also in Maricopa, in November 2012.

Among other civic-minded involvements, Schulte will assist with community-centered tribal programs, which target various educational and sports programs for youths. Plans are to provide a safe environment for Native American youth and instill in them positive attitudes through academics and sports.

Although the cost for women to play in major tours is prohibitive for most, according to Roger White, president of Native American Marketing Enterprises, Ak-Chin provided half of the $45,000 Schulte needed in 2012 to cover travel, memberships, and other fees.

She has also gained sponsorship from other corporations: Database Dynamics; BIOflex Magnetic Systems; First National Bullion, and others. Although golf is important to Schulte and she hopes someday to compete with the world's top-ranked golfers on the LPGA Tour, in December 2010 she also earned a bachelor's degree in communications.

EXTRA: THE AK CHIN INDIAN COMMUNITY

Located in the Santa Cruz Valley in southern Arizona, the Ak-Chin Indian Community is 58 miles south of Phoenix, in northwestern Pinal County. It has more than 770 enrolled members.

Its holdings include the Southern Dunes Golf Club, Ak-Chin Farms, Harrah's Ak-Chin Casino Resort, and is reputed to be one of the largest farming communities in the country.

The community has also acquired the 320-acre Southern Dunes 18-hole links course (2010), and in 2012, *Golfweek* named it one of the best resort courses in the country.

XII.
AND THOSE WITH WINGS

Two who climbed the heights...

134 Eula Pearl Carter Scott (1915-2005), Aviator

- Was the youngest person ever to fly solo, and youngest licensed pilot in the United States

Born in Marlow, Oklahoma, near the Chisholm Trail to George W. Carter and Lucy Gibson Carter, Eula Pearl's mother was an original enrollee of the Chickasaw Nation.

Curious and adventurous by nature, by age twelve, Eula Pearl had already learned to drive a car.

She met famed aviator, Wylie Post, when he landed his plane in a field near Marlow sometime in the late 1920s. Post was impressed by her intelligence, curiosity, and daring, and by age thirteen, under his instruction, not only had she learned to fly, she became the youngest licensed pilot in the United States. On September 12, 1929, she also became the youngest pilot ever to make a solo flight.

Afterward, she worked as a stunt pilot and performed until she married, became a mother, and ended her flying career to focus on home and family.

In the 1970s, Scott became one of the first community health representatives for the Chickasaw Nation, and in 1983 was the first woman elected to the Chickasaw Nation Tribal Legislature.

She served three terms and also helped to oversee the enormous growth in tribal services and operations.

Scott held memberships in the Marlow Chamber of Commerce, VFW Auxiliary, OX5 Aviation Pioneers, and the United Methodist Church.

Her life is the subject of the movie, *Pearl*, a Chickasaw Nation production based in part on the biography, *Never Give Up: The Life of Eula Pearl Carter Scott*, by Dr. Paul Lambert.

She was inducted into the Oklahoma Aviation and Space Hall of Fame; Chickasaw Nation Hall of Fame; International Women's Air and Space Museum Hall of fame, and was a charter member of the National Museum of the American Indian.

The History of Aviation Collection on Women at Texas University, Dallas contains a complete file of her aviation experiences. She was listed in *Personalities of the South* (1978-1979 edition) and *Outstanding Women of America* (1989-1990).

On the sixtieth Anniversary Celebration of Wylie Post's trip around the world, Eula Pearl Carter Scott was guest of honor and homecoming queen.

---

135 ELIZABETH (BESSIE) COLEMAN (1893-1926), STUNT PILOT

- First American of any gender or ethnicity to earn an international aviation license

Bessie Coleman was born in Atlanta, Texas and was the tenth of thirteen children. Her parents, George (Cherokee heritage) and Susan Coleman were sharecroppers. When she was two years old, the family moved to Waxahachie, Texas, and lived there until Bessie was twenty-three years of age.

At age six, she attended a segregated one-room school where she loved reading and excelled in mathematics. After completing all eight grades, she continued to attend church and harvest cotton in season. But her life would change dramatically.

Her father left Texas where he found the racial climate

unbearable for people of color and returned to Oklahoma—known then as Indian Country—where he hoped to find better opportunities. Bessie's mother and the children stayed behind.

Coleman became a member of the Missionary Baptist Church at age twelve, and at eighteen, used money she had saved to enroll in the Oklahoma Colored Agricultural and Normal University. After only one term, finances depleted, she returned home.

At age twenty-three, she moved to Chicago and lived with her brothers while she worked as a manicurist. It was there that she first heard pilots who had returned from World War I speak about flying airplanes.

The vision enthralled her, but because of her race and gender, she was unable to find a flying school that would accept her. When *Chicago Defender* newspaper editor, Robert S. Abbott, heard about her desire to pilot an airplane, he connected her with the French Flying School.

Bessie seized on the chance. To learn the language, she enrolled in a French course at the Berlitz School in Chicago, and on November 20, 1920 sailed for France.

On June 15, 1921 she became the first American of any gender or ethnicity to earn an international aviation license from the *Fédération Aéronautique Internationale*.

She became quite a media sensation and was admired by many across racial lines as she performed daring stunt maneuvers and advertised for the Firestone Rubber Company. Coleman also hoped all the publicity and contacts would help her to open her own flying school.

But Bessie Coleman's dream would go unrealized. On April 30, 1926, while she and her mechanic, William D. Willis, took her airplane for a test run before a Memorial Day exhibition, the plane developed engine problems. It went into a nosedive. Not wearing a seatbelt, she was ejected from the airplane. Willis, still inside, died on impact.

In 1995, nearly seventy years after her untimely death, a commemorative stamp was commissioned to honor her contribution to aviation.

XIII.
A SAINT,
MINISTERS, AND
GOSPEL SINGERS

THEY "WALK TO THE BEAT OF A DIFFERENT drummer" as they proclaim the Jesus Way (Christianity), while they also take pride in their Native American Indian identity.

136 KATERI TEKAKWITHA
(1656-1680)

- First Native American Indian to be declared a saint by the Roman Catholic Church

Born in the Mohawk village of Ossernenon (near what is now Auriesville, New York), of an Algonquin mother and a Mohawk father, Kateri Tekakwitha was orphaned at four years of age when smallpox took the lives of her parents and brother, left her badly scarred and with extremely poor eyesight.

Following the epidemic, her entire village was burned. Adopted by an uncle, she moved with her new family to the community of Kahnawake, and for the first time, saw Jesuit priests—men the people called "Blackrobes." Their mission was to win as many Native American Indian people as possible to the Catholic faith.

Tekakwitha's uncle, however, despised Christianity. Fearing her uncle's anger, for many years she only watched the Jesuits as they engaged in their work. But in her heart, she harbored a secret desire to become a baptized Christian.

After she was baptized, she spent long hours praying and talking to God. She also remained single and, because her friends and neighbors did not understand such a decision, was held in contempt.

Children laughed and threw stones at her each time she strayed from her uncle's longhouse. In the village, Kateri was referred to, in derision, as "the Christian," and "the Algonquin."

Life in her village became unbearable for her, and others sympathetic to Kateri's desire to live her faith and learn more about it helped her to flee to LaPrairie, Québec, Canada. Once there, she decided to become a nun.

The priests advised that she should wait until she was more mature to make such a decision, but she convinced them she was ready, and was accepted as a mission sister.

In 1680, she contracted tuberculosis and died from the disease. Those with her stated that after her death, she was transformed into a very beautiful woman, and that all of her scars disappeared.

She was venerated by Pope Pius XII in 1943 and beatified in 1980 by Pope John Paul II. Known as the "Lily of the Mohawks", Saint Kateri Tekakwitha, Virgin, was canonized on October 21, 2012 by Pope Benedict XVI.

Kateri Tekakwitha is the first Native American Indian to be declared a saint by the Roman Catholic Church. Her feast day is July 14. She is the patron saint of the environment and ecology.

---

137 Judy Jacobs, Minister, Singer

- Internationally renowned gospel artist
- Hosts her own television program, *Judy Jacobs Now!*

The daughter of sharecroppers Johnson and Gaynell Jacobs, Judy Jacobs (Lumbee) was born in Lumberton, North Carolina, and is the youngest of twelve children. The family, devout Christians, struggled financially.

Judy began singing in church at age six, and at eight under-
went a spiritual conversion experience. Her parents recognized
her talents and encouraged her toward a music career. She and
her sisters formed a gospel-singing group, The Jacobs Sisters.

She attended school in Orrum, North Carolina, population 79
at the 2000 census. She graduated from Orrum High School, entered the work force as a bank teller, and advanced to branch manager. Having sung with a number of successful gospel groups over
the years, however, Jacobs realized that music was her true calling.

In 1989, she went solo with her career and established
His Song ministry. She quickly became a staple in Gospel music
and Christian circles, with name recognition throughout the
United States and worldwide.

Unashamed of her Native heritage, Jacobs infuses Native
American Indian rhythms in songs such as the stirring call to revival, *Rain Dance*, and is known for other gospel hits, including
Days of Elijah. Because she did not have a mentor in her life for
many years, Jacobs also recognizes how crucial mentors are in the
lives of young women in choosing the right paths in life.

Through her *International Institute of Mentoring*, she provides training for those who are establishing orphanages, churches, and schools.

In 2001, with support from her husband and partner, Jamie
(with whom she has two daughters), Jacobs established the wom-
en's yearly conference, *Press...Push...Pursue*, which encourages
audiences out of their comfort zones as it encourages women to
follow their dreams at any age.

Topics explored include *Overcoming Past Mistakes and Taking
Hold of the Future; Finding Your Calling and Fulfilling Your
Destiny;* and *Mentorship: Finding a Mentor and Mentoring Others.*

Also involved in charities, Jacobs provides clothing for Native
American children and for children in orphanages worldwide.
She is host of her own television program, *Judy Jacobs Now!* that
reaches 51 million households around the world.

Some who have attended her ministry concerts and confer-
ences have reported that bodies have been healed and marriages
restored, while others report having grown spiritually and made

positive life-changing decisions.

Judy Jacobs' music albums include *I Feel a Change,* and *Above and Beyond.* She is author of *Stand Strong, Don't Miss Your Moment, Take It by Force!* and other publications.

Her performances of *Rain Dance* and others Gospel favorites can be viewed on YouTube.

---

138 THE JODY BROWN INDIAN FAMILY GOSPEL SINGERS

- Teen-aged Stephanie Brown wrote all of the songs on the album, *Possibilities*
- *JBIF Songs* reached the Top Ten

Based in Robbinsville, North Carolina, the Jody Brown Indian Family (JBIF) recorded on the Crossroads label.

Jody Brown, baritone, played bass guitar (and was the group's bus driver). His wife, Donna, sang alto, Jeremy, their son, bass, and also played the guitar and mandolin.

Their youngest daughter, Stephanie, a mezzo-soprano, also played the mandolin, and Jeremy's wife, Ashley, sang soprano. The group was renowned for its incorporation of progressive and traditional Southern Gospel with a touch of Bluegrass.

While still in her teens, Stephanie's songwriting talents were credited for much the group's success, although she co-wrote some songs with her father, mother, and sister-in-law, Ashley. She wrote all of the songs on the album, *Possibilities.*

In a 2007 *Gospel Music Today* interview, Stephanie Brown stated that her inspiration came from her parents who took her to gospel concerts while she was still an infant, and that her gospel-singing grandparents inspired her to begin to sing at a very young age.

A majority of the group were members of the Eastern Band of Cherokee Indians and to honor their heritage, in each concert they performed some of their songs in the Cherokee language.

According to the Crossroads website, the group began singing together during the early 1990s and by the mid-2000s, had several Top 10 radio hits on *Singing News* charts.

Where Is Your Faith? peaked at no. 22 (2003) and *Life is Good*, their most successful song, peaked at no. 5 on *Singing News* in the spring of 2004. *God Writes Our Story*, arguably their best album, was released later the same year.

Two of the songs from that album, *Nothing's Too Hard for God* and *Jump Out of the Boat*, peaked at no. 10 (2005).

The group's last top 20 song, *God Is Great*, from their CD album, *Come Ride with Me*, peaked at no. 15 in 2006. In 2007, they performed other hit songs that included *It Still Excites Me* (21), *Mad Mary* (59), and *Come Ride with Me* (80).

JBIF was nominated for the *Singing News Magazine* Horizon Group Fan Award (September 2000) and was honored to sing at Lee University for the Klaudt Indian Family scholarship presentation (May 2004).

As they became weary of traveling the road, they retired as a group in 2007, mostly to the North Carolina mountains. Jody and Donna Brown still perform locally. Stephanie married Dale Scragg, a former member of Karen Peck and New River Band, and moved with him to West Virginia.

The Jody Brown Indian Family music is available through Amazon on audio CDs and MP3 downloads.

---

139 Yvonne Saint Germaine, Multi-award-winning Gospel Singer

- She sings and shares her hope story throughout Canada and the United States

"My burden and goal is to reach the people in your community who are lost to addiction or abuse."

—Yvonne Saint Germaine

By her own account, prior to July 26, 2006, seven-time Aboriginal Gospel Award winner, Yvonne Saint Germaine, led a life that was "dark, lonely, abused, suicidal." Her addictions included alcohol, prescriptions pills and crack cocaine.

Her turning point, she states on her website, came when "demons began revealing themselves in my home." Yvonne knew then that if she were to survive and conquer her addictions, she would need help. She sought it through attending a pilgrimage at Lac Sainte Anne, Alberta. When the prayer line formed, she followed it forward and cried out to God.

"I felt the hand of Jesus touch me...an instant miracle took place...I was instantly set free from the bondage I was in. I never experienced detox or withdrawal."

Since the life-altering experience, Yvonne dedicated her life to telling "all who are seeking hope that Jesus saves."

A single mother of three sons, the Cree singer's pastor and his wife are influential in her ministry, where Saint Germaine provides hope through praise and worship in song and on the guitar.

She believes that the most important gift parents can confer on their children "is planting within them the seed of Jesus Christ."

Her music business, incorporated in 2010, and of which she is its sole proprietor, reflects her beliefs. A self-proclaimed evangelist, she travels to many isolated, poverty-stricken Aboriginal communities where, she states, "there is much loneliness and pain."

Saint Germaine further states that the purpose of her website is "To encourage anyone who is held in the bondage of addiction, abuse, or has lost hope." She sings and shares her hope story throughout Canada and the United States and further states on her website, "I truly believe that what the Lord has done for me He will also do for you."

She facilitates workshops, speaks on her life of addictions and abuse, and sings and speaks in schools, jails, churches, gospel tents, banquets and conventions. "Wherever the Lord gives the opportunity to let people know there is hope," she states.

Three of her original songs were at the top of the Saskatchewan and National Aboriginal charts: *Stay*, *Hand in Hand*, and *Tennessee Sky*, among others.

Her albums include: *On My Way to Heaven*; *The Hand of Jesus*;

Turning My Day Around; and *My Jesus I Love Thee*.

Among her many honors are the Aboriginal Peoples Choice Award; Best Gospel CD (2007-2008, 2009-2010); a Gospel Music Association Covenant Award; Aboriginal Song of The Year (2010-2011); and Spirit Wind Records USA Award for Outstanding Contribution to Aboriginal Music (2010-2012).

In 2010, Saint Germaine became the first female gospel artist to open at the Native American Music Awards (Niagara Falls, New York). In 2011, she won the Native American Music Award for Best Inspirational/Gospel CD; and was a 2011/2012 nominee for the Saskatchewan Country Music Awards.

She has also been the opening singer for renowned evangelist, Kenneth Copeland, and country music artist, Julian Austin.

Downloadable music can be accessed through iTunes Amazon.com, CDBaby, and other outlets.

140 CHERYL MARIE ARGUELLO (B. 1959), MINISTER

- Founder, Cornerstone Rescue Mission

Cheryl Arguello (enrolled Rosebud Sioux tribal member) was born in Cheyenne, Wyoming, to Frances H. (Thin Elk) Audiss, enrolled member of the Rosebud Sioux Tribe, and Irving Audiss, of English/Swedish descent. Of her five brothers and four sisters, she is the eldest daughter.

She attended school in Rapid City, South Dakota and by the time she completed eighth grade, Cheryl's life, marked by chaos and turmoil, began to spiral out of control. She became involved in drugs and alcohol, and by age sixteen, gave birth to a son. Confused about what to do with her life, she left Rapid City and joined Job Corps, where mentors helped her to change the direction of her life.

Although now a Christian, while growing up, her family did not attend church. Her paternal grandmother, however, would sometimes take her and her siblings with her on Sundays, and it stirred in Cheryl a desire to know the Christian God. Two years after joining Job Corps, she enrolled at Brainerd Indian School and attended Bible college. For Cheryl, it was the beginning of peace and structure in her life, but there were more challenges to come: the death of a brother, her son, and more recently, the death of her father. There was also the life-altering experience of a divorce. Through it all, she credits her faith for having sustained her.

With her present husband, Tito Arguello, Cheryl has experienced the joy of rearing six of their ten children along with six grandchildren and one great-grandchild.

Cheryl also enjoys serving with Tito at the Pierre Lakota Chapel. Affiliated with the Wesleyan Church, it had been closed for five years when she and Tito moved to the area in 2010.

Attendance now averages between thirty-five to fifty worshipers—fairly large for a Native American Indian congregation— many of them children. New families visit regularly.

During the severe winter of 2010 when Sioux families were without sufficient fuel and food to see them through, Tito braved the frigid temperatures to assist He Sapa New Life Native American Ministries (an outreach of the Wesleyan Church). Workers loaded and drove trailers and trucks to distribute needed firewood, food, and other necessities crucial for individuals and families to survive.

During the 2010-2012 Christmas seasons, Lakota Chapel targeted their outreach to the Horse Creek, Eagle Butte, and Pierre communities. During the first year, the mission's toys and gifts reached close to two hundred adults and children.

The following year, Lakota Chapel nearly doubled that number in the three communities, while He Sapa New Life was able to present the Christmas story to five additional Native communities in Rapid City, Mission, Martin, Cherry Creek, and Allen.

During the summers, Lakota chapel and other churches send work teams to help with repairs of properties and assist other outreach services where needed. Lakota Chapel also hosts a one-day event in the Horse Creek Community where the children enjoy a carnival event of singing, Bible stories, and their favorite, a bouncy castle. Morris Church (Kansas) has assisted with the event for the past two summers.

During the summer of 2010, the work team—all members of Bikers for Christ—provided motorcycle rides for everyone, a favorite of local youngsters.

Cheryl and Tito believe that personal connections with the community are key elements in building bridges to establish and maintain relationships with the people they serve. She further believes that presenting God's word is best demonstrated when the words are backed up by positive actions.

With only five more classes to complete through the Wesleyan Church's Fellowship of Leaders Acquiring Ministerial Education (FLAME) program, Cheryl Arguello expects to join the ranks of the very few Native American women who are ordained ministers.

When her busy schedule allows it, the familiar figure in Pine Ridge and other Native communities still indulges her love for making star quilts, a traditional Lakota skill she learned from her mother (See Lakota Quilters).

EXTRA: WESLEYAN CHURCH SUPPORT

The Wesleyan Church supports not only the Pierre Lakota Chapel where Cheryl Arguello and husband Tito serve, but other outreaches to Native Americans.

Wesleyan also acknowledges publicly that, although their motives were noble, over the generations, their ways of sharing their faith and interacting with Native Americans were greatly flawed.

In 1998, they offered an apology which is posted on their website.

More: The Wesleyan Church's Apology

We have seen and been told that our Native American brothers and sisters "have something against us." We as a denomination, organization, or individuals cannot go back and undo what has been done. We can, however, seek forgiveness and reconciliation from our brothers and sisters today. You may not feel comfortable accepting this reconciliation on behalf of all your people, but would you accept it as an individual?

As a member of the dominant race, I acknowledge many sins of the past done by my people. My people took the land without regard to the rights of those who had been its inhabitants for many generations. We destroyed the food sources and left you no choice but to accept handouts. We took the best land for ourselves and gave you, our brothers and sisters, what we felt was of no value. When we discovered there was value in some parts of what we said you could have, we took that back as well.

We took your children--often by force--to "teach" them. They were forced to change their language, hair, dress customs, and cultural identity. These sins not only affected your ancestors, they have been carried for generations. The anger and frustration this loss has caused each successive generation has never been resolved or reconciled. The end results of these feelings have surfaced many times in the forms of substance abuse, suicide, and family violence.

As a denomination I ask you to forgive The Wesleyan Church. We are at the altar knowing we need to have the wrongs of the past forgiven and reconciled before we can continue in complete fellowship with God the Creator. We believe the first Wesleyan missionaries followed the Gospel of Jesus Christ by coming to the Native American people. In trying to present the message of love and salvation, they wanted to follow a pattern that was, at that time, considered effective, and ultimately followed what had been done by other denominations and the federal government. However, we feel the pattern they followed was not the right one. In our Wesleyan schools and churches, we, too, forced you to change your language, songs, hair, dress, customs, and cultural identity.

Wesleyans have individually and corporately opposed the discrimination against and exploitation of Native Americans. Although not all Wesleyans have maintained proper attitudes, our voices have been repeatedly lifted on behalf of our brothers. We have made mistakes in evangelism and discipleship when dealing with cultural issues. We believe these errors were based more on people's limited cultural understanding than their bad hearts, and grew out of a zeal for righteousness that we misguided in its application. It was an error repeated around the world at that time by nearly all religious groups. It was an error we, as a denomination, deeply regret.

As individuals we also must leave the altar and seek your forgiveness. We are, too often, guilty of looking at Native Americans as a "needy" people without looking at the great number of things you have to offer us. We are guilty of wondering, "Why don't they just do things our way?" We seldom take time to see the great worth of your views; how you incorporate worship into every area of life; value the wisdom of the elders; revere family relationships, music, song; instill the virtues of bravery, fortitude, wisdom, generosity; and perceive ownership of land.

As a race, a denomination, and as individuals, please forgive us for the sins of our forefathers, our denomination, and our individual sins against you. Please forgive us, forgive me. God forgive us all.

ABOUT THE AUTHOR

ALTHOUGH SOUTH FLORIDA-BASED CHEROKEE/ Seminole heritage author KB Schaller is primarily a novelist who writes about Native characters at spiritual crossroads, she has long nurtured the idea of a biographical collection that honors Native American women.

As a guest blogger on a number of sites, and on her life's journey, what she has discovered haunts her: while mainstream Americans have heard of larger-than-life historical figures such as Geronimo, Crazy Horse, and others, besides Pocahontas and Sacajawea, they are largely unaware of the accomplishments and contributions of Native American women.

While Pocahontas and Sacajawea rightfully hold their places in history, Schaller has longed to share a much broader field of historical and contemporary women of Indigenous heritage whose contributions deserve to be recognized.

"I welcome the opportunity to harvest information scattered here and there and compile it into a single volume. I hope it will be inspirational to all who are interested in viewing Native American women, not as exotic curiosities, but accomplished, dynamic and many-faceted human beings."

Also a conference speaker, independent journalist, artist and poet, Schaller also states that compiling, editing and adapting *100+ Native American Women Who Changed the World* was a daunting task. "It kept growing and growing. Ideas kept pouring in." So many that she was obliged to add the + to the title.

The research was so consuming, she put her third novel in her *Journey* series on hold. She further acknowledges that although *100+*, her first Native-themed non-fiction work includes some compiling of facts and figures, it strives to reach beyond that to "incorporate the human element of our oneness, and to make it more interactive."

She further describes the experience as a lesson in itself, an honor, an enlightening, humbling challenge that gave her different perspectives on life and the passing of time. Her only regret, she admits, is that there are "thousands more" intriguing and accomplished women of Indigenous heritage who deserve inclusion that time and space did not permit.

Schaller is a member of the Native American Journalists Association, Cassell Network of Writers/Florida Freelance Writers Association, LinkedIn, Florida Publishers Association, and the Tallahassee Writers Association.

In addition to professional writers organizations, KB Schaller holds memberships in Chickee Church on the Seminole Indian Reservation; National Museum of the American Indian; Ah Tah Thi Ki Museum of the Seminole Indian; and is an honorary committee member of the American Indian Education Foundation, among other affiliations.

She is also a published poet, and her paintings have won Best in Show and other distinctions.

Schaller's debut novel, *Gray Rainbow Journey*, is a *USA Book News* -National Best Books Award winner, and winner of a Florida Publishers Association President's Best Books Award.

The sequel, *Journey by the Sackcloth Moon*, continues to explore the angst of a Native American beauty caught between two worlds, two loves, two faiths.

Journey Through the Night's Door, third in the series, is in progress. She collaborated on a screenplay based on *Gray Rainbow Journey*, and is seeking a producer.

http://www.KBSchaller.com

REFERENCES

Abernathy, Jesse, *Pine Ridge Reservation Still Among Poorest*, Before It's News website, January 25, 2012

Aboriginal Peoples' Choice Awards 2012, *Mary Youngblood, First Lady of the Flute*

About.com website, Military History, *Invasion of Normandy*

About Me website, *Colleen Swan*

Admin., NativeNewsToday.com, *Alexandrea Schulte Finishes in Top 20 on Ladies Golf Tour*, May 4, 2012

African American World, *Edmonia Lewis*

Akatubi Film and Music Academy

Alcatraz Is Not an Island, Timeline of Indian Activism website

All-Athletics.com, Sun Devil Athletics Cross Country official website

Allen, Lee, *Grammy Nominee Radmilla Cody Up for Three Native American Music Awards*, Indian Country Today Media Network, May 7, 2013

Alpha Pi Omega official website

American Indian Encyclopedia, *Leslie Marmon Silko*

American Indian Heritage Month, *Native American Women Veterans*

American Indian Science and Engineering Society, *Otakuye Conroy-Ben*

Americans for Indian Opportunity, *LaDonna Harris*

Ancestry Message Board (Obituary), *Charlotte Edith Anderson Monture*

Annual Gathering of Nations Powwow 2012, *Women's Fancy Shawl*

Answers.com, American Authors, *Joy Harjo*

Answers.com, *Mary Youngblood*

APB American Program Bureau, *Winona LaDuke*

Arguello, Cheryl Marie (Submitted Biography)

Arizona State University Office of General Counsel, *Diane Humetewa*

Arlington National Cemetery, *Gertrude Simmons Bonnin* (Zitkala-Sha, Red Bird), Army Spouse

Athletics site, Sun Devils Arizona State University, *Alvina Begay*

Artist Direct website, *Mildred Bailey*

ASK website, *Ann Curry*

Ault, Jon, The Spanish-American War Centennial Website, *Native Americans in the Spanish American War*

Baker, Judy (Submitted Biography)

Bellafaire, Judith, PhD, Curator, *Women in Military Service For America Memorial Foundation, Inc.,* History@womensmemorial.org (Native American Women Veterans)

Betty Mae Tiger Jumper obituary

Betty Mae Tiger Jumper website

Beyal, Duane, *Navajo Fashions* (VirginiaYazzie-Ballenger)

BiggestStars.com, Biography (Irene Bedard)

Biography.com, *Coleman Hawkins*

Bio.True Story:
Bessie Coleman
Lewis and Clark
Maria Tallchief
Sacagawea
Susan LaFlesche Picotte
Wilma Mankiller
Women in History (Edmonia Lewis)

Biography of Women Mathematicians website (*Freda Porter)*

Blackard, David M., and West, Patsy, *Seminole Clothing*
http://www.semtribe.com/Culture/SeminoleClothing.aspx

Blogger News Network, *The Native American Nurses of the Spanish-American War*

Blue Ridge Country magazine, *The Beloved Woman, Nancy Ward*

Bonner, Jessie L., *Law Professor Building Native American Program,*
July 27, 2009 powwows.com website

Bonners Ferry Herald Online, *Amelia "Amy" Cutsack Trice, 75,* Obituaries,
Thursday, August 4, 2011

BookRags website:
Diane Glancy biography
Janet McCloud

Boswell, Evelyn, MSU News Service, *Montana team more than performers at 1904 World's Fair,* May 04, 2004

Boulard, Garry, Diverse, *Native American Law and Order: Angelique EagleWoman, Law Professor*

Brannum, Juliana, director, *LaDonna Harris, Indian 101 30-Day Challenge!*

brendanorrell@gmail.com, Censored News, *Salvage,* directed by Sheila Tousey and written by Diane Glancy, Friday, September 12, 2008

Briggs, Kara, *Cherokee Rocket Scientist Leaves NMAI a Gift,* Muskogee Phoenix, December 15, 2008, www.muskogeephoenix.com

Bronitsky and Associates, *Virginia Yazzie-Ballenger,* www.bronitskyandassociates. com/wordpress/

Browse Biography, *Annie Dodge Wauneka*

Brudvig, Jon L., Ph.D., *Hampton Normal and Agricultural Institute: American Indian Students (1878–1923)*

Cabe, Delia, *World Beaters,* Humanities, November/December 2010, Volume 31, Number 6 (Fort Shaw Girls Basketball Team)

California State University, Fresno Peace Garden, *Anna Mae Pictou Aquash*

Canadian Association for the Advancement of Women in Sports and Physical Activity, Milestones, *Sharon and Shirley Firth,* 2011

Canadian Encyclopedia, the, *Tantoo Cardinal*

Canadian Ski Hall of Fame, the, *Sharon Firth, Shirley Firth*

Canadian Ski Museum, *Sharon Firth, Shirley Firth*

Canada2010.gc.ca, *Sharon and Shirley Firth*

Celebs.Bio, *Glancy, Diane*

Cemeteries of Seattle, Princess Angeline

Cerveri, Doris, *Dat-So-La-Lee, Queen of the Basket makers*

Changing the Face of Medicine, Biography, *Dr. Susan LaFlesche Picotte*

Chickasaw Nation Hall of Fame, *Eula Pearl Carter Scott*

Chips Quinn Scholars Program website

City of Kivalina website, *Welcome to Kivalina!*

Climate Guest Blogger, Colleen Swan and Christine Shearer, *Drilling in the Arctic: Perspectives from an Alaska Native,* October 7, 2011

Cody, Radmilla Official Homepage

Colorado Progressive Jewish News, Rob Prince's Blog, *Eugenics: Partial Bibliography on the Involuntary Sterilization of Native Americans in the 1970s,* September 28, 2011

Conroy-Ben, Otakuye (Submitted Biography)

Cordova, Randy, *Musician's life is a rich tapestry,* The Arizona Republic (AZCentral.com), February 8, 2012

Cox, Melanie (contributor), *Wright, Laura, Obituaries of Alaska's Pioneers as extracted from End of the Trail, beginning April 5, 1997*

Crossroads, *Details about Jody Brown Indian Family* (JBIF)

CUBIT, Kivalina City Census, 2010 Data

Dance Magazine, Inc., *Oklahoma salutes its five Native American ballerinas,*1998

Darlene McCarthy Ministries website, *Judy Jacobs* (biographical data)

Department of Civil and Environmental Engineering, University of Utah, *Otakuye Conroy-Ben*

Deseret News, *Leader of last American Indian war dies at 75,* Friday, July 29, 2011

Dictionary of Literary Biography on Diane Glancy

Dictionary of Literary Biography on Ella (Cara) Deloria

D'Oro, Rachel., Huff Post Green Internet Newspaper, Kivalina, Alaska, *Eroding village appeals lawsuit's dismissal, blames corporations for climate change,* January 28, 2010

EduQnA.com website, *Why do some people when they jump down or parachute shout "Geronimo"?*

Edwards, Stephanie, Maria Martinez website (Prezi transcript), January 11, 2013 (Dr. Edgar Lee Hewett)

EHow, *History of Seminole Indian Dolls*

Emory University English Department, *Leslie Marmon Silko*

EMusic website, *Radmilla Cody*

Encyclopedia of World Biography, *Sacagawea,* Copyright 2004, The Gale Group Inc.

ENotes, *The Man to Send Rainclouds* (Leslie Marmon Silko)

Exton, Brother Benet, O.S.B., Book Review, *Father Francis Craft, Missionary to the Sioux,* by Thomas W. Foley

Faculty Profiles, University of Utah, *Otakuye Conroy-Ben*

FamousPoetsAndPoems.com, *Joy Harjo*

Fandango, *The Broken Chain,* (Buffy Sainte-Marie)

Fandango, *Smoke Signals*

fashionfinds.com, *Echoes of the Pueblo* (Patricia Michaels)

Fashion Windows, *Patricia Michaels Fall 2010: Inspired by the Majestic Eagle,* New York, February 14, 2010 http://www.fashionwindows.net/2010/02/patricia-michaels-fall-2010/

Film Reference, *Buffy Sainte-Marie biography* (1941–)

Find a Grave Memorial #821, Record added: Jan 01, 2001 (Pocahontas)

FirstAmericans.org, *Native American Actresses, Irene Bedard*

Five Moons, the

Flickr (from Yahoo), *Sharon Irla's Photostream*

Fold3 Person Page, *Laura Belle Beltz Hagberg Wright,* Haycock AK. 22 February, 1996

Free, Kalyn (Submitted Biography)

Free Library by Farley, the, *Coaching Goal of Champs* (retired skiers Shirley and Sharon Firth)

Frida Kahlo Fans, *Brief Biography*

GaDuGi website

Gease, Heidi, *Rios Pleads guilty to accessory in Aquash murder, given suspended sentence,* Rapid City Journal, November 8, 2010

Gersh-Nesic, Beth, *Artists in 60 Seconds: Edmonia Lewis,* About.com, Art History

Giago, Tim, *When Leader Charge Spoke, Kevin Costner listened,* Indianz.com, Monday, April 2, 2012

Give Your Everything Canadian Olympic Team website, *Mary Spencer, Boxer*

Glancy, Diane (Submitted Biography)

Globalsecurity.org, 207th Infantry Group (Scout)

Golder, Julie, Bonners Ferry Herald Online, *Porter passionate about education, Kootenai culture,* November 23, 2011

Graf, Mercedes, *Women Nurses in the Spanish American War*

Great Falls Tribune.com website, MontanaCana, *Heart Butte rancher was first Native American female in the U.S. Marines* (Minnie Spotted Wolf)

Green, Sara Jean, *Portraits of a Princess: Iconic images of Chief Seattle's eldest-daughter on display, The Seattle Times Company,* Friday, July 13, 2001

Griffin, P. Joshua, Episcopal News Service, *Standing with Kivalina at the 77th General Convention,* June 29, 2012

Gun and Game, *Laura Beltz Wright*

Hampton, David, *Association of the Descendents of Nancy Ward, Biography of Nancy Ward*

Harbsmeier, Debbie, WHAS 11.com, *TLC to debut documentary on Shoni Schimmel,* May 3, 2011

Harjo, John, Canku Ota, *The Naomi Lang Story,* January 26, 2002

Hey Doc website, *The Native American Sisters of the Spanish American War*

Hickman, Kenneth, *Battle of Oriskany,* About.com (military history)

HistoryLink.org, Essay 9512, *Christine Quintasket* (Mourning Dove)

Hoffman, Lisa, *Indian women celebrated as unsung heroes,* Scripps Howard News Service, May 25, 2003

Holy Bear, Charlene (Submitted Biography)

Hoopedia, *Fort Shaw Indian School*

HubPages, Haunted Lake View Cemetery, Seattle, *Princess Angeline, Daughter of Chief Seattle*

HUD.gov, *Native American Women in the Military*

ICTMN Staff, *Native American Kootenai leader walks on*, July 25, 2012

ICTMN Staff, *Navajo Alvina Begay Hopes to Represent U.S. as Olympic Marathoner*, October 29, 2011

ICTMN Staff, *Sold-Out Nike N7 Sport Summit Aims to Advance Native Youth Access to Sport*, October 25, 2011 (Alvina Begay)

IMDb:
    Dome of Heaven, The
    Doris Leader Charge
    Irene Bedard (film credits)
    Kivalina Vs Exxon, 2011

IMDbPro:
    Apache 8
    Tantoo Cardinal biography

Indian Life, *Coeur d'Alene Tribe seeks recognition for famed jazz singer* (Mildred Rinker Bailey), May-June 2012

Indianz.com, *Shoni Schimmel, Umatilla Basketball Star*

INDN's List Facebook page

Info Please All the Knowledge You Need website, *Irene Bedard, Actor, Singer*

Iowa Public Television website, *For the Rights of All: Ending Jim Crow in Alaska* (Alberta Schenck)

Irla, Sharon Fine Art website

Jazz.com, *Bailey, Mildred* (Mildred Rinker)

Jawort, Adrian, *Mariah Watchman: Native Supermodel in the Making*, ICTMN, April 24, 2012

Jean, Terri, Editor, The Native Truth, Manateka American Indian Council, *11 Native Americans Everyone Should Know* (Patty Talahongva)

Johnson, Peter, greatfallstribune.com website, *Heart Butte rancher was first Native American female in the U.S. Marines* (Minnie Spotted Wolf)

Journal staff, *Ola Mildred Rexroat served as a WASP in World War II*, Wings Wasp website, Thursday, May 21, 2009

Judy Jacobs Ministries website, personal biography

Kahlo, Frida, Paintings by

Kateri Center, the, Kateri's Life

Keefe, Julia, Reality Now 2012, Nez Perce Tribal member #4152, Frost School of Music, Class of 2012, *Bailey and Native American Jazz*, posted March 24, 2012 http://realitynow2012.wordpress.com/2012/03/24/mildred-bailey-and-native-american-jazz/.

Kivalina, Alaska website

Knight Center for Specialized Journalism Archive, Patty Talahongva

Lakota Funds Economic Resurgence Report, the, *Murdock Electric Lights Up New Markets on Pine Ridge Reservation,* Spring 2012

Lakota Funds Staff biography, *Tawney Brunsch*

Lakota Star Quilts website:
https://m.facebook.com/page/about.php?id=226545185750&__user=1036143968
http://aktalakota.stjo.org/site/News2?page=NewsArticle&id=8594&news_iv_ctrl=0

Quilters:
Bell, Ernestine Joyce
Brave, Regina
Good Lance, Vera
Moves Camp, Germaine
One Feather, Leola
Two Bulls Weasel Bear, L. Pansy
Thin Elk, Wilma

Lammers, Dirk. Seattlepi.com, *Canadian appeals conviction in '75 AIM slaying,* Monday, March 19, 2012

Laskaris, Sam, Indian Country Today Media Network.com, *Hoop Dancing Dynamo Lisa Odjig from Canada's Got Talent,* April 29, 2012

Leizens, Tish, *Young Native Golfer Alexandrea Schulte Now Golf Ambassador of Ak-Chin Tribe,* Indian Country Today Media Network.com, August 16, 2012

Leizens, Tish, *Thunderbird American Indian Dancers,* Indian Country Today Media Network.com, January 21, 2013

LeValdo, Rhonda (Submitted Biography)

Lewis, Jone Johnson, About.com guide, *Edmonia Lewis*

Literari.net, About the Author, *Leslie Marmon Silko*

Locate Grave website (Julia Helen Nashanany Reeves)

Logan, Joe, Knight-Ridder Newspapers, Orlando Sentinel, *Back from the Brink to the Rink,* July 2, 1989 (Tai Babilonia)

Louisville.com, *Louisville's Shoni Schimmel at White House Today,* June 20, 2012

Lumbee Regional Development Association, *Alpha Pi Omega Sorority*

Manataka American Indian Council, Women's Circle website, *Beloved Woman of the Cherokee, Nancy Ward c. 1738–1824*

Manta, Where Small Business Grows, *Lakota Funds*

Manta, Where Small Business Grows, *Murdock Electric and Maintenance Company*

Maria Martinez and San Ildefonso Pottery webpage

Marston, Muktuk, *Men of the Tundra: Alaska Eskimos at War, excerpt, Chapter 11, The Beam in Thine Own Eye,* 1969, 1972 (Alberta Schenck)

Martin, Linda R., *Navajo Style, Fashion for All Seasons* (Virginia Yazzie-Ballenger)

Maynard Institute, Native American History Month, *Mary Hudetz*

McAnulty, Sarah, *Angel DeCora: American Artist and Educator*

McCarthy, Darlene website, *Judy Jacobs*

McGuigan, Patrick B., *Oklahoma's Kalyn Free Closes INDN's List, Saying 'Yakoke' (Thank you),* The City Sentinel, December 30, 2010

McNeel, Jack, Today Correspondent, *The Kootenai Tribe's Forgotten War,* August 24, 2010

Messina, Irene, *A new documentary tells the story of an all-female Apache fire-fighting crew,* Tucson Weekly, March 24, 2011

Michaels, Patricia, h2owaterlily@gmail.com website

Miller, John, Getting Out, *Jazz Singer Mildred Bailey Returning to Tribal Roots?*

Minnesota Indian Women's Sexual Assault Coalition, MIWSAC

Montana History Wiki, Outstanding Montanans, *Susie Walking Bear Yellowtail*

Moremus, David, *The Real Pocahontas* (Irene Bedard)

Motions Online, *Angelique EagleWoman*

MSU News Service, *Montana team more than performers at 1904 World's Fair*

Mudhooks, Shorpy Website, *Charlotte Edith Anderson,* Tuesday, February 2, 2010

Museum of Contemporary Native Arts (MoCNA)

Museums USA, *Museum of Contemporary Native Arts* (MoCNA)

Native American Encyclopedia, *Princess Angeline, Duwamish,* Published by Amy, May 2, 2012

Native American Encyclopedia, *Wilma Mankiller Achievements,* March 9, 2011 (published by Carol)

Native American Journalists Association (NAJA) website

Native American Rights Fund website, *John E. Echohawk*

Native Americans: Friends or Enemies? Timeline of Indian Encounters with Jamestown Colonists (1607-1679) website (Pocahontas)

Native American Women Veterans, The first record of Native American Veterans website: https://www.facebook.com/NativeAmericanWomenWarriors/info- Spanish American War Nurses: http://www.spanamwar.com/NativeAmericans. htm.

Native American Women Veterans:
  Bailey, Bernice(Firstshoot), Corporal
  Bordeaux, Susan
  Clarke, Ella
  Fletcher, Alida Whipple
  Monture, Charlotte Edith Anderson
  Pleets, Anna
  Reeves, Julia, First Lieutenant
  Rexroat, Ola Mildred
  Sinnard, Cora
  Spotted Wolf, Minnie, Private
  Thayer, Beatrice Coffey
  Two Bears, Josephine
  Wale, Elva Tapedo

Native Networks:
  Rae, Heather
  Tousey, Sheila

Navajo Spirit Southwestern Wear, *Virginia Yazzie-Ballenger*

Native Voices 1969 website, *Indians of All Tribes group occupies Alcatraz Island*

NC Gives, *Alpha Pi Omega Sorority*

Nelson, Valerie J., *Elouise Cobell dies at 65; Native American Activist,* the Los
  Angeles Times, October 17, 2011

Nevada Women's History Project (NWHP): *Dat So La Lee*

Native American Veterans

Newberg, Julie, Media Relations, ASU, *Diane Humetewa*

Newseum Institute website: http://www.newseum.org/

Newspaper Rock, *"Superstar" Native Basketball Player,* January 28, 2011

New World Encyclopedia, *Other Topics* (Ft. Shaw Girls Basketball)

New York Amsterdam News, *Mary Golda Ross: The First Native American
  Female Engineer*

Nike N7 SportsSummit, October 28–30, 2011

North Dakota Office of the Governor website, *Rough Rider Award:* http://www.
  governor.nd.gov/theodore-roosevelt-rough-rider-award

NOW website, *Native American Women and Violence,* Spring 2011

nurses.info, *Susie Walking Bear Yellowtail, 1903–1981*

Ojibwa, Native American Netroots, *American Indians as Slaves*

On All Frontiers, Four Centuries of Canadian Nursing website, *Charlotte Edith
  Anderson*

OneidaIndianNations.com website, *Tyonajanegen*

Ongtooguk, Paul, *Veterans of the Tundra: Territorial Guard Helped Reduce Alaska Racism,* Alaska Dispatch, November 11, 2011

O'Shea, Ciaran, IMDb, *Mini Biography, Sheila Tousey*

Oxendine, Tasha, *Lumberton woman spreads the Gospel around the world,* Native Visions Magazine blog, March 1, 2007 (Judy Jacobs)

Partnership for Progress, Minority Banking Timeline, *Elouise Cobell,* 1987

Peavy, Linda and Smith, Ursula, *Full-Court Quest,* University of Oklahoma Press, 2008 Fort Shaw Girls' Basketball Team:
Burton, Minnie
Butch, Genie
Healey, Genevieve
Johnson, Belle (Captain)
Langley, Josephine (Organizer)
LaRose, Rose
Lucero, Flora
Mitchell, Sarah
Sansaver, Emma
Snell, Katie
Wirth, Nettie

Peavy, Linda and Smith, Ursula, *Full-Court Quest* (Winslow, William, M.D.) University of Oklahoma Press, 2008

Phillips, Aron, Film Premiere, *Off the Rez Is Hoop Dreams Meets Glory Road,* April 27, 2011

Phillips, Patsy (Submitted Biography)

Pictou Maloney, Denise, Counterpunch.org, *The murder of our mother, Anna Mae Pictou-Aquash,* May 18–20, 2007

Pitts, Byron, *Native American Women Veterans Celebrate President's Inauguration,* CBS Interactive, Inc., Pueblo West, Colorado, January 21, 2013

Polar Ice Gilbert official website, *Naomi Lang, Instructor*

Prentice, George, *Native American Who Waged 'War' Against U.S. in Idaho dies,* Boise Weekly, August 1, 2011

Publications and Research, *Lorelei DeCora*

Publishers Weekly, Editorial Review, *Waterlily*

Racebending.com, *Tantoo Cardinal, Actress*

Rain, Erica, *IMDbPro, Hanbleceya, a Plot Summary* (Georgina Lightning)

Randy'L Hedow Teton website

Rapid City Journal, *Otakuye Conroy will become the first Lakota to earn a doctorate degree in environmental engineering,* March 25, 2006

Rapid City Journal, *12 in 12: Meet the Journal's 12 to Watch in 2012* (Tawney Brunsch), January 1, 2012 (interview)

Read Periodicals, *Apache 8*, April 1, 2012:
Cheryl Bones
Erica Hinton
Katy Aday
Nina Quintero

Reality TV Games, *Tai Babilonia* (Professional)

Reference.com, *Anna Mae Pictou-Aquash*

Richardson, Marilyn, *Finding Edmonia Lewis and Others*, ArtFixDaily.com, January 9, 2011, updated May 10, 2011

Rickert, Levi, editor-in-chief, Native Currents, Native News Network, *Color Guard at White House Tribal Nations Conference*, posted April 30, 2013

Ritten, Sandra, *Shoni Schimmel Takes College Basketball by Storm*, Indian Country Today Media Network.com, February 11, 2011

RoadsideAmerica.com, Your Online Guide to Offbeat Tourist Attractions, *Monument to World's Greatest Girls Basketball Team of 1904*

Romeo Institute website, *Madonna Thunderhawk, Organizer and Tribal Liaison*

Roy, Anusha, KXLY 4 Reporter, *Prominent Northern Idaho Tribal Leader (Amelia Trice) Dies*, September 08, 2011

Rutecki, Gregory W., MD., Center for Bioethics and Human Dignity, Trinity International University, *Forced Sterilizations of Native Americans: Late Twentieth Century Physicians Cooperation with National Eugenics Policies*, October 8, 2010

Rutherford, Lynn, special to icenetwork.com, *It's an August ice dance wedding weekend*, August 22, 2008 (Naomi Lang)

Rutherford, Lynn, special to icenetwork.com, *Lang, Tchernyshev enjoy overseas opportunities*, November 08, 2010

RWJF website, *Lorelei Decora*

Sabalow, Ryan, *A long history of loss for Pit River Tribe*, redding.com, September 17, 2011

Seminole Indian Dolls website

Seminole Patchwork website

Saint Germaine, Yvonne, official website

Schaller KB, *Apache 8 Female Firefighters a 'First'*, Christianpost.com /bindings, August 14, 2012

Schaller, KB, *Lori Piestewa, A Memorial Day 'First'*, Christianpost.com /bindings May 30, 2011

Schaller, KB, *Osama Bin Laden, Geronimo, and the Native American Perspective*, Christianpost.com/bindings, July 08, 2011

Schaller, KB, *Seminoles' First Female Chief Walks On*, Indian Life, March-April 2011

Schaller, KB, *Susan LaFlesche-Picotte,* Indian Life, March-April 2013

Schilling, Vincent, *Native American Women Warriors celebrate inauguration while raising awareness for Native female veterans,* Indian Country Today Media Network.com, January 21, 2013

Schulte, Alexandrea, *About Alexandrea,* (Facebook)

Scott, Gregory, *The Legendary Oklahoma Aviator,* TulsaPeople.com, June 2009

Seattlehistoryblog.com, *Princess Angeline,* March-April, 2011

Seminole Legend, Betty Mae Jumper, a, February 2011 (obituary tribute)

semtribe.com/bettymae/index.shtml, *Betty Mae Jumper, A Seminole Legend*

semtribe.com website, *Seminole Patchwork*

Share the Inner Sanctuary website, *Navajo Spirit Southwestern Wear-Share and Tell*

Sharp, Jay W., *Profile of an Apache Woman,* Desert Resource website

Short, Candy Franklin, Encyclopedia of Oklahoma History and Culture, *Marjorie Tallchief*

Silko, Leslie Marmon, http://www.english.emory.edu/Bahri/Silko.html

Silver Wave Music, *Mary Youngblood*

Silver Wave Records, *Mary Youngblood*

Smith, Captain John, *The Settlement of Jamestown –1607*

S9.com, Biographical Dictionary (Babilonia, Tai Reina)

Snow, Patricia Gabbett, Albuquerque Journal, *Grandmother Walked in Velvet* (Virginia Yazzie-Ballenger), Thursday, August 1, 1997

Sovereign Oneida Nation of Wisconsin website, *Oneida Healers, Hospitals, Doctors & Nurses*

Speakers.com, *Tai Babilonia*

SpeakOut! website, *Madonna Thunderhawk, Community Organizer in Native America*

Spirit People Intertribal Family, *Women of All Red Nations*

Starkman, Alvin, M.A., J.D., *Women Potters of San Marcos Tlapazola, Oaxaca* ezinearticles.com, Arts and Entertainment>Humanities, March 3, 2009

Stephens County Archives, *Eula Pearl Carter Scott*

Stern, Ray, *Obama squeezes out first female Native American U.S. Attorney; Diane Humetewa submits resignation,* Valley Fever, July 28, 2009

Super Lawyers website, *Keith M. Harper*

SuperiorPics.com, *Celebrity Profiles* (Irene Bedard)

Takeuchi, Craig, *WFF 2011: Alaskan village battles power giants in climate change documentary, Kivalina v. Exxon,* Straight.com website

Theater for the New City website, *Thunderbird American Indian Dancers*

thechurchonline.com, *Judy Jacobs*

Thigpen, David E., *Kevin Costner Said the Words but Doris Leader Charge Made the Dances Dialogue Truly Sioux,* People magazine, January 21, 1991: http://www.people.com/people/archive/issue/0, 7566910121,00.html

Till, Dustin, Turtle Talk website, *Legal Analysis of the Kivalina v. Exxon Case*

Tirado, Michelle, *INDN's List Closes Its Doors*, American Indian Report, December 21, 2010

Tisch School of the Arts website

Today in History, *Sarah Winnemucca*, October 14, 2010

Today@UCI, University of California, Irvine, *Wilma Mankiller, Cherokee Nation leader and Presidential Medal of Freedom recipient, to address UC Irvine Rainbow Festival,* Thursday, November 2, 2006

Today website, *Ann Curry*

Trainer, Marsha, IMDb, *Mini Biography, Georgina Lightning*

UltimateDisney.com Presents *An Interview with Pocahontas*, May 11, 2005

University of Idaho News website, *Sharon Eagleman, Champion Jingle Dress Dancer,* April 13, 2011

U.S. Army Medical Department, Office of Medical History website, *Answering the Call to Duty: Native American Nurses*

usgwararchives.org, Obituaries of Alaska's Pioneers, *Laura Beltz Wright, as extracted from End of the Trail*

Voices from the Gaps, University of Minnesota:
Diane Glancy
LaDonna Harris
Zitkala-Sha

Wasserspring, Lois, *Oaxacan Ceramics:*
http://www.google.com/search?tbo=p&tbm=bks&q=inauthor:%22Lois+Wasserspring%22

Waugh, Frank Albert, *Wauneka, Annie Dodge,* American National Biography Online

Welcome to NAMA Live website, *Radmilla Cody* (Winner, 2013 NAMA, Best Record, *Shi Keyah-Songs For the People*)

Wentworth, Karen, *LaDonna Harris and Americans for Indian Opportunity Collection opened for scholars*

Wesleyan Church Native Ministries website, *Our Apology for Past Cultural Insensitivity*

What-When-How, In Depth Tutorials and Information, *Eskimo Scouts*

White, Julia, *Dahteste, Mescalero Apache*

Whitefield-Madrano, Autumn, *The Evolving Beauty of the Fancy Shawl Dance*, Indian Country Today Media Network.com, March 20, 2011

Whitman, Kurt, Motions Online, *About Professor Angelique EagleWoman*, March 23, 2011

Williams, Jasmin K, *Mary Golda Ross: The First Native American Female Engineer*, New York Amsterdam News, March 21, 2013

Women in Mathematics website, *Freda Porter, Mathematician*

www.squidoo.com/Lozen

www.missamerica.org/our-miss-americas/1920/1926 (Smallwood, Norma Descygne)

Women in History (Edmonia Lewis)

Youngblood, Mary website

WIKIPEDIA.ORG REFERENCES

Addelman, Ben; Alaska Territorial Guard (ATG)
Alpha Pi Omega Sorority
Angeline, Princess
Aquash, Anna Mae
Bailey, Mildred
Babilonia, Tai
Bedard, Irene
Bird, Jackie
Boarding Schools, Native American
Brown, Jody, Indian Family
Cardinal, Tantoo
Carlisle Indian School
Cobell, Eloise
Cody, Radmilla
Coleman, Bessie
Counting Coup
Curry, Ann
Dahteste
Dances with Wolves
Dat So La Lee
De Cora, Angel
Deloria, Ella Cara
Dove, Mourning
Durham, Jimmy
Eberhardt, Aubrey
Echohawk, John E.
Eskimo Scouts
Five Moons, The
Geronimo
Golda Ross, Mary
Goodacre, Glenna
Harjo, Joy
Harris, LaDonna
Hewett, Edgar Lee
Holt, Thaddeus
Hoop Dance
Humetewa, Diane
Irla, Sharon
Jingle Dress Dance, Native American

Jumper, Betty Mae Tiger
Kahlo, Frida
Kivalina, Alaska
Kootenai Tribe of Idaho
LaFlesche Picotte, Susan
Lang, Naomi
Lewis and Clark Expedition
Lightning, Georgina
Mankiller, Wilma
Martinez, Maria
Miles, Douglas
Naismith, James
Neil, Lilakai Julian
Norvo, Red
Odjig, Lisa
Peltier, Leonard
Pickner, Jasmine
Piestewa, Lori Ann
Rae, Heather
Ross, Mary Golda
Rough Rider Award
Sacagawea
Sainte-Marie, Buffy
Silko, Leslie Marmon
Smallwood, Norma Descygne
Smoke Signals
Saint Germaine, Yvonne
Talahongva, Patty
Tallchief, Maria
Tallchief, Marjorie
Tekakwitha, Kateri
Teton, Randy'L Hedow
Tousey, Sheila
Tyonajanegen
Uintah and Ouray Tribe
Ward, Nancy
Women of All Red Nations (WARN)
Zitkala-Sha (Gertrude Simmons Bonnin)
Zoom Info

INDEX

"Render therefore to all their dues: tribute to whom tribute is due...honour to whom honour."
—Romans 13:7

TITLES BY KB SCHALLER:

NON-FICTION:

100+ Native American Women Who Changed the World

FICTION:

Gray Rainbow Journey, Winner, USA Book News-National Best Books Award; Florida Publishers President's Best Books Award for Young Adult Fiction

Journey by the Sackcloth Moon (sequel)

Journey Through the Night's Door (coming soon)

ACKNOWLEDGMENTS

The following persons and organizations are deeply appreciated for their assistance, suggestions, and encouragement:

- Carolyn Kingcade, a sister by blood and spirit, who has followed my writing career faithfully, and rendered indispensable assistance and support.
- Carole DiTosti, PhD, for unselfish assistance in promoting the works of many.
- Candace Begody, *Navajo Times*, for suggesting candidates for this publication.
- Those who have hosted me on their blog sites: Diane Stephenson, Elaine Stock, Tom Blubaugh, Lisa Miller-Chandler, Diane Lesire Brandmeyer, and *Bindings* (christianpost.com).
- Dana Cassell, writers.editors@gmail.com, for support in so many areas.
- Lenzy Krehbiel-Burton, Grand Director, Alpha Pi Omega Sorority, for her research assistance and suggestions for candidates.
- *Native American Public Telecommunications* (NAPT) for posting my call for nominees on their website, and for posting links to my blogs that were of interest to Native America.
- Thanks to Michael Kelly and Ron Looking Elk for placing me in contact with key individuals who greatly impacted the outcome of this work in a positive way.
- Heartfelt thanks to the following for their prayers, encouragement, and support: my husband, Jim; members of our prayer circle; *LinkedIn* friends who offer support and promotion for writers.
- Cassell Network of Writers; Tallahassee Writers Association; Florida Publishers Association; and "fan club" members (especially my Aunt Thelma), who have read, commented on, and passed on my titles by word-of-mouth.
- My thanks (and apologies!) to any whose names I may have, without intention, omitted.

CPSIA information can be obtained
at www.ICGtesting.com
Printed in the USA
BVHW030447190919
558880BV00001B/79/P